Just Passing Through
Notes from a Sojourner

Just Passing Through

NOTES FROM A SOJOURNER

Margaret Guenther

SEABURY BOOKS
an imprint of Church Publishing, Incorporated, New York

The following originally appeared in *The Christian Century* on the dates
given and have been revised for this volume by the author: "Touch and
See" (April 12, 1995); "So—What Was the Question?" (April 19, 1995);
"Sheep" (April 26, 1995); "If only you would…Yes, but…" (May 10,
1995); "Bad Math" (May 17, 1995); "Midnight Mystics" (May 24–31,
1995); "In Defense of a Woman Named Martha" (July 5–12, 1995).
© 1995 Christian Century Foundation. Reprinted with permission of
The Christian Century. Subscriptions: $49/yr. From P.O. Box 378, Mt.
Morris, IL 61054.

The following originally appeared in *The Vintage Voice* in a slightly different form: "Reflections of a Septuagenarian"; "A Secret Word"; "Notes
from a Sojourner." They are reprinted with permission.

"Holy Agnosticism" is an edited and expanded version of an essay/arti-
cle that appeared in *Episcopal Life* in 1999. Reprinted with permission.

Library of Congress Cataloging-in-Publication Data
Guenther, Margaret, 1930– .
Just passing through : notes from a sojourner / Margaret Guenther.
   p. cm.
  ISBN-13: 978-1-59627-050-3 (pbk.)
  1. Guenther, Margaret, 1930– . 2. Christian biography—United
States. I. Title.

BR1725.G946A3 2007
283.092--dc22

2006033111

Cover design by Vicki K. Black.
Cover photograph: © Marco Secchi / Alamy

Church Publishing Incorporated
445 Fifth Avenue
New York, NY 10016

Printed in the United States of America.

07 08 09 10 11 12   10 9 8 7 6 5 4 3 2 1

Contents

GROWING OLD

WORK

LIFE GOES ON

Acknowledgments

I am grateful to my editor Joan Castagnone for her sensitive and generous support during the writing of this book.

Since we do not know who wrote the Psalms, that great book of songs and prayers, I have referred to the author(s) simply as the Psalmist. Quotations from the Psalms are from the 1979 *Book of Common Prayer* of the Episcopal Church. All other scriptural quotations are from the New Revised Standard Version, unless otherwise noted.

All language about God is limiting, for God is infinitely beyond our comprehension. For convenience in the pages that follow, I have used traditional language—that is, the masculine pronoun—fully aware that the loving Creator God is Father, Mother, and much much more.

As always, I am indebted to Jack, my follow sojourner of nearly half a century.

*This book is dedicated
to the memory of Otto, my father.*

Sojourning

Much as I admire the scholarship that has given us the New Revised Standard Version of the Bible and much as I rejoice in the painstaking accuracy of the translation, I lament the loss of a few wonderfully poetic, admittedly archaic words.

No longer do we read of *sojourners*. These folk have become "resident aliens" and "passing guests." As a sojourner myself and as someone whose best friends are sojourners, I would like to reclaim that word in all its depth and promise.

It is an Old French word with *jour* (day) at its heart. It reminds us of our transience and of the inexorable passage of time. It reminds us of our smallness and ultimate powerlessness. It reminds us that we do not own this world but are merely passing through. It reminds us that God's time is not our time.

The Ninetieth Psalm is the prayer and song of the sojourner:

> Lord, you have been our refuge
>   from one generation to another.
> Before the mountains were brought forth,
>   or the land and the earth were born,
>   from age to age you are God.
> You turn us back to the dust and say,
>   "Go back, O child of earth."

For a thousand ages in your sight
    are like yesterday when it is past
and like a watch in the night.
                    (Psalm 90:1–4)

The reflections that follow are the ruminations of a sojourner.

Prodigality

For the LORD your God is bringing you into a good land, a land with flowing streams, with springs and underground waters welling up in valleys and hills, a land of wheat and barley, of vines and fig trees and pomegranates, a land of olive trees and honey, a land where you may eat bread without scarcity, where you will lack nothing.

(Deuteronomy 8:7–9a)

God and Purple Loosestrife

A few years ago on a bus ride through New England I saw my first purple loosestrife. The summer meadows were spectacular, an undulating sea of spiky reddish-purple flowers. It was a visual feast, an excess of purple, a color that most decorators would use cautiously and sparingly. I couldn't get enough. As we rolled toward Newburyport, I wanted the little journey to go on forever.

Later I asked a local friend, "What is that *gorgeous* flower I saw in all the fields between here and Boston?" He looked at me with thinly concealed disgust and replied, "That's loosestrife." His tone suggested that I was maybe too naive to be let out on my own, that maybe I wouldn't be able to distinguish between a Norway rat and the Easter Bunny. His tone also suggested that "loosestrife" was a naughty word, almost an expletive. A little poking around the encyclopedia told me that this Old World marsh herb, now naturalized in the eastern United States, is regarded by farmers as invasive, noxious, and downright abhorrent. You rarely talk about it in polite society, and you most certainly do not admire it.

So I went underground. My love of this beautiful flower became my guilty secret, to be enjoyed from train and car windows but not flaunted to the locals.

I was therefore surprised last summer to see pricey pots of purple loosestrife on sale at our local garden shop. It lost some magnificence by being confined in nondescript plastic containers alongside the geraniums and impatiens, those reliable standbys of city gardeners. But restrained as it was, it was unmistakably the extravagant loosestrife of the summer meadow. "Can you actually sell this?" I asked the shop's proprietor. "I thought it was banned along with other controlled substances." He reassured me: this loosestrife was specially bred and guaranteed sterile. It would provide a magnificent splash of purple in my backyard but would be denied the gift and heritage of children.

That was last year. This year we have twice as much exuberant loosestrife, and there are tiny plants popping up everywhere. Our purple loosestrife, despite the assurances of Mr. Johnson, has turned out to be a promiscuous plant. I still love it, maybe love it even more because it refuses to be restrained. Its very name suggests abandon, prodigality, indeed a certain wildness that is lacking in my North European/Anglo-Saxon/Midwestern/middle-class being. As the deer longs for the water brooks, my soul yearns for the extravagance of purple loosestrife, maybe also for the equally prodigal thistle, beloved of goldfinches and despised by thrifty farmers.

It's so easy to second-guess God. It's so easy to forget that God created quite a few species that most of us would prefer s/he had left in the planning stage. Even as I am willing to co-exist with most snakes and actually like bats, I would happily forego garden slugs and mosquitoes. We might also hint to God that sometimes a little can go a long way, so that we could manage happily with less of some varieties. Out in Jenkins Hollow this has been an exceptional summer for poison ivy. Glossy, dark green leaves cover the old stone walls and fan out lavishly along the roadside. It is as beautiful as my loosestrife, but I find myself thinking that if I were God, I'd cut down on the poison ivy and encourage the wild grapes. They don't make anyone wild with itching, and they provide food for the foxes and raccoons.

In my more honest moments I can recognize my hubris. Speciesism—I discovered to my surprise that it is an honest-to-goodness word in the dictionary—is just one more ugly little "ism," maybe less virulent than racism, sexism, and ageism. But like all our ugly little "isms" it is based on selfish, limited judgment. It is an ongoing surprise to realize that my idea of what is good and worthy does not necessarily coincide with God's. It is unsettling when I am forced to realize, yet again, that God refuses to be confined by me, anymore than my promiscuous purple loosestrife could be confined in its plastic pot.

Quite a few years ago I was guest preacher in a parish that was still uneasy at the sight of a woman in the pulpit. I should have kept out of trouble, but by chance or graced coincidence, the gospel for that Sunday was the story of the Prodigal. It's amazing that I survived coffee hour, perhaps that I was not stoned as I left the parking lot. I had pointed out something in that familiar story that most of us (including me) manage to forget most of the time: the prodigal is not the wayward, wastrel son. The true prodigal is his recklessly extravagant father.

In a society that carefully guards property and property rights, this father has simply handed over a sizeable fortune to a greedy and irresponsible child. This father—before he has time to hear the story, while the

delinquent and disappointing son is yet at a distance—
runs to embrace him and kisses him. This dignified
property owner of mature years runs to hug someone
who has been living in a pigpen. And, although he has
no more disposable wealth since the remaining share
belongs by right to the elder son's inheritance, this
father orders lavish gifts and plans a big party. He gives
away what isn't his anymore.

This was more than that congregation of exemplary
elder brothers (and sisters) could bear to hear. Maybe
they had hoped that the story would turn out differ-
ently on this particular Sunday morning. Maybe they
had hoped that this time their carefulness and hard
work would be praised. They didn't like what they
heard from me, even though they had no doubt heard
it many times before.

Sometimes I think that we fail to realize the absurdity and the exuberance of this story because it's just too
much for us. Most of us, even when we are not quite
so self-righteous as the elder brother or so guilt-ridden
as the younger, are more comfortable with a God who
runs a taut ship. We'll obey—or break—all the rules
and then wait for God to deal with the delinquents. We
have our standards of what is useful and what is not, of
who is worthy and who is not. A proper deity should
also have standards and exercise restraint.

I'm still trying to get my mind around the prodigality of God. That might be an impossible task because it
is quite beyond my limited left-brain. The God of purple loosestrife and glossy poison ivy is the God who
doesn't always play fair, at least by my standards.

The overwhelming excessiveness of creation pales
compared to the prodigality of God's love. This is love
lavished with abandon and, by my standards, with poor

taste. This is the God who pays the last-minute slackers the same wage as the hard-working folk like me, the ones who show up early and skip their lunch break. This is the God who then has the temerity to ask, "Am I not allowed to do what I choose with what belongs to me? Or are you envious because I am generous?" (Matthew 20:15).

This is the God of thistles and purple loosestrife, the God of bats and garden slugs. This is the Prodigal God who overwhelms me with his prodigality.

Feeding the Multitude

The housewife in me loves the stories of Jesus feeding the four thousands and the five thousands (not counting women and children). The gospel writers must have loved them too since all four gospels include at least one version (Matthew 14:13–21, 15:32–39; Mark 6:30–44, 8:1–10; Luke 9:10–17; John 6:1–13). I can read these stories symbolically, as a prefiguring of the institution of the Eucharist, but most of the time I read them as real stories of real people who needed to be fed. That's a story I can relate to.

Goodness knows, there are plenty of times when I have put together a giant casserole of tuna, noodles, and canned soup to feed an unplanned multitude. It's not an elegant dish, but it's better than nothing. Maybe because she was feeding a fair-sized family during the Depression, my mother was even more creative than I. Her greatest achievement of making something out of nothing happened when I was about eight. We returned from a brief vacation to find the front porch full of distant cousins from Illinois. They had just dropped in for a visit—a visit of several days, of course. It was a hot August Sunday, and the stores were closed—this happened in olden times before malls and round-the-clock supermarkets—but somehow she produced an abundant meal out of nothing.

Jesus doesn't complain, but it seems to be a recurring experience for him: just when he thinks he has removed himself from the crowds for a little rest and reflection, all those people turn up. Or else they are waiting for him when he arrives. I can imagine that he and his friends sometimes felt stretched to the limit, probably felt that they had nothing more to give. And then the crowds, like the Illinois country relatives of my childhood, are lying in wait for him, confident that he will be glad to see them.

This happens often in the gospels: Jesus can't get away. People are clamoring to be near him—to hear his teaching, to be healed, just to be with him. So the crowd is waiting for him when his little boat arrives. And it's a big crowd—five thousand men! Matthew's version of the same story adds "not counting women and children." This would increase the number drastically and might also explain where the baskets came from. Women are always carrying things.★

As I picture the scene, it's been a long day of hot sunshine, and Jesus and his friends are surrounded by a teeming mass of all sorts and conditions of people. I'm pretty sure that they are not all nice, polite people. I suspect that they have come with a variety of motives, histories, and needs. There are probably even a few con artists and pickpockets in the crowd. Could there have been souvenir sellers? Maybe. Maybe it was something like a big, fairly peaceful gathering on the Washington Mall on a summer day.

When Jesus saw this great throng, he "had compassion on them because they were like sheep without a shepherd." In other words, he saw them as aimless, lost, and without clear purpose. So—no matter how he was

---

★ I am grateful to Megan McKenna for this insight, eloquently set forth in *Not Counting Women and Children: Neglected Stories from the Bible* (Maryknoll, NY: Orbis Books, 1994).

feeling—he was able to put himself aside and to be present to them despite his own fatigue and concern.

The mother/housewife in me can imagine what the scene was like at the end of the day, after people had listened for hours to his teaching. The babies were crying, tempers were growing short, and there were a lot of people with headaches and growling stomachs. The disciples are practical: it's getting late, they say. It makes sense to send them off to get something to eat.

There follows a stunning example of the unreasonableness of Jesus, his way of calmly asking, indeed commanding the impossible: you go ahead and feed them. The disciples' response: with what? Where are we going to get enough money to buy what it would take? We don't have anything—except. . . .

Except some little bits of bread and a couple of fish. Except. . . . We don't really have anything. Except. . . . Just enough for ourselves. Not enough to make any difference. What we have doesn't count for much. We don't have anything. Except. . . .

But Jesus turns to his friends—and when I put myself in the story, I know that he is turning to me— and asks: How many loaves do you have? What do you have that I can work with? What do you have that we can—together—use to pull off a miracle? How can we manage some holy sleight of hand that will baffle the literal-minded for millennia?

It is easy to forget the humble stuff of miracles, the materials readily at hand: bread, the simplest, most basic food, and a few dried fish. If the story were taking place today, there would probably be some day-old Wonder bread and bargain-priced generic tuna, the kind that's just a jump ahead of catfood.

Yet despite the appearance of poverty and meager-ness, the result is startling abundance. Everyone is fed. The five thousand and presumably the women and children have eaten their fill, and there are baskets of leftovers.

This is a story about real people—earthed, embod-ied, and physical. Jesus knows that people get tired and hungry and that they must be fed. In other words, he recognizes our neediness, along with our very human limitations, especially the sad fact that we are not natu-rally generous. I can picture myself standing among his friends, avoiding looking him in the eye as I mumble: I haven't anything anyone would want, really nothing worth giving. I haven't anything you could use. Except. . . .

He is willing to wait for my answer, to wait for as long as it takes for me to look into my lunch box or brown bag or elegantly outfitted picnic basket, only to discover that there is a lot more in there than I had realized. It may not look like much, but it is the stuff of miracles.

Bad Math

Let everyone who is thirsty come. Let anyone
who wishes take the water of life as a gift.
(Revelation 22:17)

What beautiful absurdity! These words from the
Revelation to St. John, almost the very last
words of our Bible, set me thinking about God the
accountant, God the mathematician, God the economist. In other words: in ways I don't usually think
about God.

There is a powerful message encoded in our culture:
everything must add up. From the earliest days of our
formal education, we are taught to sneer at the absurdity that two plus two *might* equal five. I still remember,
after the passage of quite a few decades, the laborious
tedium of drilling into my brain: two plus two equals
four. Only the dullards would come up with five or
three. Or try to defend their position. Discussion and
dissension were not encouraged in our humble little
school: this was a fact, this was to be memorized, this
was the way it was.

Throughout our lives we go on making things add
up, making sure the sides of the equation are equal. In
my days as teacher/administrator, I kept a calculator in
one desk drawer and a Bible in the other; and in the
course of an ordinary day I was equally likely to whip

out the calculator, just to make sure that things added up and that that holy document—the budget—was being honored.

We insist that everything must add up because we know that everything has a cost and we know all too well that resources are limited. That is, our material resources can be measured, meted out, and sooner or later exhausted. So we have our cynical clichés: You get what you pay for! There's no such thing as a free lunch! Unexpected generosity is frequently greeted with suspicion, for all too often gifts have strings attached and are not true gifts. Wisely, we learn to be wary of promises of no down payment, the "free gifts" advertised on television, the dream of something for nothing.

Everything has its price. In our shop windows, numbers and dollar signs seem to be our chief decorative symbols. We learn to beware of restaurants so elegant that the prices are not printed on the menu. And, rich or poor, we all, to some degree, cultivate the art of getting the most for our money. Two decades of living in New York made me an expert practitioner, with zest for the game even when it didn't really matter.

Not surprisingly, we are impatient with those who do not pay their way or "pull their weight." So society's "gift" of welfare assistance to its poorest and most helpless is a grudging one at best, and we are merciless with the cheaters (those who cannily or cynically beat the system) when they are caught.

Yet these words of the exiled John on Patmos are a part of joyous vision of consummation and restoration, a picture of *Shalom*—that peace of God that is wholeness, harmony, and right relationship. These words are a clear echo of the fifty-fifth chapter of Isaiah, that other song of homecoming and invitation to abundance:

> Ho, everyone who thirsts, come to the waters;
>   and you that have no money,
>   come, buy and eat!
> Come, buy wine and milk
>   without money and without price. (55:1)

Both exiles offer a picture where two plus two does not necessarily equal four, indeed where nothing adds up—at least not in the way I absorbed in Miss Shannon's second-grade classroom.

So let everyone who is thirsty, come. Remember though: you have to be truly thirsty, not just mindlessly taking in, consuming for the sake of consumption. This invitation is issued to the spiritually alive, which may rule out some people whose physical vital signs are in order, but who don't yet know about the thirst for God.

Jesus knew about thirst—the ordinary thirst of those living in a hot climate and the torturing thirst of a man dying on the cross, and he knew about the thirst for God that enlivened the Samaritan woman, the thirst for God that the Psalmist likens to the thirst of a deer seeking a brook in the wasteland. He taught a lot about thirst and the cool refreshing water that assuages it. He taught of the blessing that rests upon the person who gives a cup of water to those who bear the name of Christ. Or, for that matter, the blessing of the gift of water to anyone who thirsts. "Lord, when was it that we saw you thirsty and gave you something to drink?" And he says: "Just as you did it to one of the least of these who are members of my family, you did it to me" (Matthew 25:37, 40).

We need water to keep us alive—literally, physically. More than that, like the Psalmist's deer and like the

Samaritan woman at the well, we thirst spiritually. We are promised, again and again, that this thirst will be assuaged. Moreover, the stilling of our thirst will be a gift. That vital, essential, mysterious, life-sustaining something is there for the taking. For free! This reminds me of play with very small children, where transactions are conducted with pretend money and prices are absurd. Two cents, a million dollars, what's the difference? Just name a number. Just pull some grown-up sounding figures out of the air. Could it be that we are dealing with a playful God? A God who says: I'll pretend with you, we'll use the vocabulary you understand, but it's really free. Pay no attention to the price list. The numbers don't matter.

It's disquieting to think that God may be right! That God's math may be better than ours!

Sometimes I wonder whether God is very interested in money, in that page in the newspaper that gives the current value of the yen, the mark, the dollar. And now the Euro. I have no doubt, however, that God is interested in our treasure—or our perception of treasure. God the economist is interested in our use and stewardship of our resources, how we spend our precious substance, the best that we have.

The prodigality of God's generosity is hard to grasp, and it's equally hard to grasp and to celebrate how rich we really are. Our society distracts us with bright and nearly empty packages, with a dazzling array of real and spiritual junk food. Our society discourages us—nothing can be free, so the kind of lavish abundance offered by a God who promises the water of life as a gift must be nonsense. Just look around you, my cynical inner voice says, where's the feast?

Most of us don't feel rich. I suspect that even rich people, that is, people whose god is their material wealth, don't feel rich, or at least rich enough to enjoy their affluence. With the late Duchess of Windsor they are convinced that you can never be too rich or too thin. Yet if we are to believe the message of Scripture and the message of Christ, there is such abundance that we can stop counting, such abundance that quantities are meaningless.

This is hard to believe. I have to confess, though, that like most of the human race I have a genius for looking in the wrong direction and missing the point completely. And I must confess too that math has never been my strong point. Maybe it's time to throw away the calculator and rethink—or repray?—my spiritual arithmetic.

Midnight Mystics

Mathematics was never my best subject. I survived secondary education by memorizing without understanding, solving problems without truly comprehending the questions, and clinging to bits of formula like a drowning person hanging on to a floating log. I made it through Introductory Algebra, uneasily, tentatively; and it never occurred to me to attempt Astronomy.

Nowadays, when I look at the night sky—the work of God's fingers, the moon and the stars God has established—I regret my limited vision. The Psalmist had a glimpse of the scope of complexity and intricacy of creation, the sheer wonder of space and time that cannot be expressed in words nor shown in pictures, but might begin to be apparent to an Einstein or a Stephen Hawking.

I knew Psalm 8 in childhood, when memorizing reams of Bible verses was rewarded with adult approval and a growing row of little stars on a chart in the Sunday school classroom. As a Midwesterner, I loved it. In those days I could not see the beauty in great expanses of wheat fields or in straight roads stretching toward the horizon. Instead, I yearned for mountains, rocks, and rushing streams. But even as I rejected my Kansas surroundings as "boring" and wished that I had been born a New Englander (if it were not possible to be Swiss or Tyrolean), I could always see God's handi-work in the sky. The Psalmist, I thought, would recog-nize and appreciate the broad sweep of our Kansas horizons and the sheer immensity of the sky.

Decades later, when I realized that my life's journey would take me to live in New York, indeed in the heart of the city, I woke in the night and wept. "I'll never see the sky again," I said to myself in the darkness; I dared not add, "I'll be cut off from God," but in my heart I knew that that was why I wept. Yet on bright winter nights, when I caught sight of a single star that some-how had managed to outshine the city lights, or when I watched the moon rise high and triumphant over Central Park, I knew that I was still looking at the work of God's fingers, even in the city.

The sight of the night sky makes mystics of us all. YHWH brought Abram outside and said, "Look toward heaven and count the stars, if you are able to count them" (Genesis 15:5). And of course he could not. Yet Abram saw something beyond his comprehension and received a promise that defied logical explanation. His grandson Jacob saw the heavens open, with angels ascending and descending. He too received a promise. The magi saw a star and followed it. We forget what a costly and perilous journey that must have been. And the shepherds were the first to hear the great news of the Incarnation when they saw the sky illumined in what must have been the greatest *son et lumière* show of all time.

It is almost as if God is saying, "Plant fields, build roads and houses, cover the earth with your little cre-ations, even pollute and deface if you must; but if you look up, you will still see the heavens, the work of my fingers, the moon and the stars I have established. Look

up, even in the middle of the crowded city with its
bright lights and murky air, which you have filled with
impurities. Pay attention, and you might see more. Pay
attention and you might see what Abram and Jacob
saw, the cosmic intricacies that drew the Wise Men
from the East. You might have a glimpse of the wondrous light that overwhelmed those grubby and unlet-
tered shepherds on the Judean hillside. Pay attention,
and you might encounter me."

Our rickety old house in the Virginia Blue Ridge is
far from any city, and there are no neighboring houses
in sight, so the night sky there approaches the clarity,
blackness, and brilliance suggested in the Psalm. There
it is my special joy to sleep outdoors, directly under the
stars, and to wait in the presence of the work of God's
fingers. Rain, of course, drives me inside; and temper-
atures below about twenty-eight degrees are too much
of a challenge. But otherwise, I pull on warm socks and
a sweatsuit and drag my sleeping bag onto the deck
over the porch roof.

People my age tend to sleep lightly, to wake and
then go back to sleep. When I lie in my sleeping bag
under the heavens, I rejoice in this easily broken sleep.
Because of it, I can almost feel the earth turn as I watch
Orion move slowly across the sky. On bright nights
there are showers of falling stars. Sometimes the scud-
ding clouds are so dramatic as they cover and then
reveal the moon I think, "This can't be real. This is an
artist's idea of light and shadow, motion and conceal-
ment." Planes fly over in predictable patterns, their
sound coming long after their tiny bright light. I wonder who is traveling through the night and try to
remember to say a prayer for them. Toward dawn, when

the sky begins to lighten, the bats fly home; and I know that my time of watching is nearly over.

Sometimes I get cold: it is not unusual to scrape frost from my sleeping bag on a winter morning. In the summer I think occasionally about nocturnal creatures and wonder if snakes might climb as high as the porch roof. I become attuned to sounds and can tell the level of the river by the noise it makes as it tumbles over the rocks. In the summer, I can tell time by the noises—the tree frogs fall silent around three o'clock, and the warblers along the riverbank don't begin to stir before five.

My family has given up worrying about me, although articles on hypothermia can stir up a little concern. I have become a legend to the locals—"So *you're* the woman who sleeps outdoors all year round, even in the winter!" I no longer try to explain what impels me; I am happy to be just one more eccentric in a neighborhood that tolerates eccentrics.

But in my heart I know what draws me to lie under the night sky. I know why I am sometimes taken by surprise, even when I have experienced it hundreds of times. I know why sometimes I am awestruck, why I almost involuntarily call aloud upon God's name. I have seen the work of God's fingers. And for a little while, I know who I am. I know my place.

Friends and Sisters

But what happiness, what security, what joy to have someone to whom you dare speak on terms of equality as to another self; one to whom you need have no fear to confess your failings; one to whom you can unblushingly make known what progress you have made in the spiritual life; one to whom you can entrust all the secrets of your heart and before whom you can place all your plans! ★

—*Aelred of Rievaulx,*
twelfth-century Cistercian abbot

★*Spiritual Friendship* (Kalamazoo: Cistercian Publications, 1977), 72.

Thank You, Betty Friedan!

Time looks different from the perspective of the eighth decade. While this vantage point doesn't quite rival that of God, of whom we sing "A thousand ages in thy sight are like an evening gone," thirty or forty years doesn't seem like much anymore. When I am with my young female colleagues and friends, I have to keep reminding myself that they take for granted what still seems startlingly new to me.

I recall the first time I heard of *The Feminine Mystique.* It was at a suburban dinner party in the mid-1960s, one of those quasi-professional gatherings where the men talked business while their stay-at-home wives diligently avoided controversial subjects that might damage their husbands' careers. So we talked about pregnancy, child-rearing, schools, and recipes. Those were the days when you did creative things with dry onion soup mix. I had said something about "the mystique of bread making"—in those days I baked all our bread—and one of the wifely huddle burst out, "Have you read it? Have you read the book?" None of us had, so she treated us to a capsule summary of what sounded like a revolutionary document. Obviously, the little word "mystique" had taken on a life of its own and, for women in my circumstances, would no longer stand alone but be forever linked with "feminine."

The next day I bought my own copy and devoured it at one sitting. I can't find it now. It may have fallen apart from age, got lost in a move, or never been returned by an unreliable borrower. It doesn't matter. I suspect that now I would find its contents tame and its message ho-hum.

But the late sixties and early seventies were a yeasty time. Women began to talk to each other, *really* talk about what *really* mattered to them. They began to look at their experience with new eyes and to ask themselves what they truly wanted, who indeed they were. Assuredly, it was a time of political awakening, but more importantly, it was a spiritual epiphany. After centuries, millennia of voicelessness, women began to find their collective and individual voices. Even for the least political among us, the slogan "Sisterhood is powerful" took on depth and meaning.

I like men. I have been married—at last count—for forty-six years to one. I am the mother of another fine man and grandmother of a promising crop of little and not-so-little boys. Some of my best friends are men.

But now I, who have no biological sisters, rejoice in the friendship and sisterhood of women. There is an ease in our conversation that would never have been possible at those highly structured dinner parties of the sixties. We're not trying to impress each other. We're not competing with each other. Maybe we are recovering some vestige of tribal bonding, lost long, long ago when we became too civilized. We still talk about cooking and children. We are still interested in clothes and like to admire each other. But we also talk about hopes and fears, life and death. We talk about men, individually and generically. And we talk about God. God the Father and God the Mother. God the Lover and God the Inexplicable Other. We tell jokes, jokes that we don't tell our husbands and sons, but that we might share with our daughters.

My sisters are a motley crew, ranging from thirty-something to ninety-something. Most of them don't know each other. I enjoy the fantasy of getting them all together some day for an extended slumber party—the warmhearted, lively group of Baptist women from Mississippi who introduced me to weaving, my Roman Catholic Benedictine sisters from Kansas, the dedicated South African women who run a center to protect their sisters from violence, my poet friend Ardyth, my Dominican friend Kathleen who has an uncanny way of knowing when I need her prayers, Mary Louise who's been my sister-in-law for more than half a century, my colleague Pattie who's young enough to be my daughter but treats me like a buddy. The list could go on and on. And since it's a fantasy party, there's no need to restrict the number of guests. We would rejoice in one another's presence, laugh a lot, and no doubt shed some tears. We would be bound together in the sisterly friendship first modeled by Mary and Elizabeth in Luke's gospel (1:39–56).

Luke doesn't say, but I always picture Mary alone when Gabriel came to her and told her not to be afraid, that the Holy Spirit would come upon her, that the Most High would overshadow her, and that she would become the mother of the holy child. The encounter ends with a short little sentence that I had overlooked for decades: the angel departed from her. She is left alone with an awesome, terrible, joyous secret—and she hastens to seek out a trusted friend.

Mary and Elizabeth are different in age, circum-stances of life, and perhaps in how they felt about themselves. Yet they are united in their friendship, their womanhood, and their fruitfulness: they are both "expecting"—to use the euphemism of my childhood. They are both the bearers of new life.

Luke tells us that Mary remained for three months and then returned to her home. What did they talk about during those ninety mornings, middays, and evenings? Did they take turns reassuring one another in times of fatigue, morning sickness, or just plain panic? Did they talk about the men in their lives— worry together about Zechariah's speechlessness and ponder what to say to Joseph when the crucial conversation could be postponed no longer? Maybe they spent long hours sitting together sewing, resting in a companionable silence. Maybe they laughed together at Elizabeth's baby's vigorous leaps that knocked her handwork off her lap. Maybe Elizabeth listened as Mary told and retold the story of her angelic visitor.

Two very different women, they were able to talk about what really mattered to them. Together they looked at their wondrous experience and realized their strength: the Mighty One had done great things for them, and holy is his name. They could afford to be humble and to accept the role of handmaids and servants. They knew who indeed they were.

Thank you, Betty Friedan, for helping me begin to know who I am. Thank you even more, Mary and Elizabeth. You show us what the feminine mystique is really all about.

The Spiritual Significance
of a Sally Lunn Cake—
Actually, Only Half of One

Last January found me in England's West Country, offering two workshops in a Roman Catholic convent. Sunday afternoon was free, as one group departed and the newcomers had not yet arrived. I was quite prepared to curl up in my room with a whodunit, but Sister Tessa insisted that I needed an outing. So we drove through the countryside to Bath. She knows and loves every stone of that old city. In her enthusiastic company, I was reminded of a bit of Psalm 102, where the Psalmist is speaking not of a beautifully preserved English city but of a desolate Zion: "For your servants love her very rubble, and are moved to pity even for her dust." I am convinced that Tessa would continue to love a Bath lying in ruins and would be moved to pity even for her dust.

But this was a glorious winter day of deep blue sky and sun shining on the honey-colored old stones. Tessa, very English, doesn't look like a nun. Indeed, I'm not sure that she even owns a traditional habit. Our hike through the city was pure fun, as if we were carefree students just now set free to discover the world rather than two staid-looking women of a certain age. Tessa knew all the stories—who had lived where, some Jane Austen lore I had not heard before, how the city had grown in layers over the centuries. With understated charm, she finagled our way into the cathedral after closing hours. Likewise after closing hours she managed access into the restroom of the elegant Pump Room. We must have looked like two Miss Marples on the loose.

Our afternoon culminated in tea in a fifteenth-century house that had been the monastery bakery until Henry VIII's destructive rampage, but it is now famous as the house where Sally Lunn had lived. She had come from France—in the seventeenth? eighteenth century?—and was the wife of a baker. That's not her real name, but it's as close as her English hosts could or would come to pronouncing her French name.

"We must have Sally Lunn cakes with our tea," Tessa announced as soon as we found a table in the low room with its heavily beamed ceiling. I'd seen recipes for Sally Lunn cake in old cookbooks and had never been tempted to try it. It just didn't look very interesting. But I was in the hands of an expert guide, so we agreed on the "Bath Cream Tea," which meant that we each got half of an enormous Sally Lunn cake spread thickly with cinnamon butter. And clotted cream on the side, of course. I looked at this huge, rich thing on my plate and told myself, "I'll have a few bites, just to be polite, and then push it around while we talk." For all sorts of reasons, mostly caloric, I try to avoid sweets.

Well! I devoured the whole half-cake. It was delicious. I savored the cinnamon butter and added some globs of clotted cream. When my plate was empty, I didn't feel guilty. I just felt very happy. I was almost purring. I knew that the memory of my buttery Sally Lunn would stay with me for a long time.

As we moved out into the winter twilight, I said to Tessa, "That was a spiritual experience." She agreed.

I found myself remembering some lines tucked in the middle of the seemingly interminable Psalm 119:

> Oh, how I love your law!
>   all the day long it is in my mind.
> Your commandment has made me wiser
>   than my enemies,
>   and it is always with me.
> I have more understanding than all my teachers,
>   for your decrees are my study.
> I am wiser than the elders,
>   because I observe your commandments.
> I restrain my feet from every evil way,
>   that I may keep your word.
> I do not shrink from your judgments,
>   because you yourself have taught me.
> How sweet are your words to my taste!
>   they are sweeter than honey to my mouth.
>   (Psalm 119:97–103)

The beginning of this passage is forbidding. I suspect the Psalmist of some insincerity, maybe an attempt to butter up the Lord with his enthusiasm for his law. Then comes the surprising analogy: the word of God is sweeter than honey in the mouth. I wondered: could my self-indulgent tea in Bath have something to do with God? Is there a message here about the lovely sweetness, the richness of the butter, the spiciness of the cinnamon? Was there even something holy about the cozy space in that ancient building? It was bustling and very twenty-first century on that winter Sunday afternoon, but I sensed that it was filled with all the friendly ghosts of people who had sat in that low-ceilinged room, eaten, laughed, and talked over the centuries. It felt as if those long-gone Benedictine bakers looked down from heaven in approval of our self-indulgence. After all, even in medieval monasteries, Sunday was a feast day. What better way could we latter-day pilgrims have found to savor God's goodness!

Although I hope to renew my friendship with Tessa and her sisters when next I am in England, I'll probably never eat another Sally Lunn cake. One is enough. I think I've had a glimpse of what the Psalmist was talking about.

Women Without Words

I know practically nothing about my German grand-mother. She died long before I was born. As I child, I visited her grave each Memorial Day, but that seemed more like a late spring outing than an act of familial piety. She was buried beside my grandfather in an old country cemetery, surrounded by wheatfields and pastures. (Now the suburbs have grown up around it, and it is an anachronistic little memorial to those sturdy old farm folk.) I was embarrassed by her name—Minnie Beltz. Walt Disney had only recently burst on the scene with the animated adventures of Mickey and Minnie, and it pained me to have a grandmother who shared her name with a cartoon character with oversized shoes, flapping eyelashes, and a squeaky voice. Only as an adult did I realize that her name was no doubt Minna, an old word that means "love."

She was born on a farm in Missouri, but never learned English. I doubt that she had much schooling, indeed probably none at all. She was a young widow with two sons when she married my grandfather. Such marriages were common in rural North America of the late nineteenth century: a farmer needed a woman on the place for all sorts of domestic duties, and a single woman with young children needed the protection of a husband. It was surely a practical, even businesslike arrangement, by no means the stuff of romantic ballads.

My father was the eldest child and only boy of this marriage. They were dirt poor. I know that my grandmother had little beauty or leisure in her life. My only legacy from her is four wine glasses, a crudely patched quilt top, and her picture. She is seated next to her husband, staring straight into the camera. Her hair is pulled back in a tight knot. Her body is stocky, and her face is round. She is not a soft or pretty woman. I realize now that she was much younger than her husband, a true patriarch with a flowing white beard. I suspect that this was her first experience of being photographed. She certainly looks terribly ill at ease, rather as if she is facing a firing squad.

I know that she was a good woman because she reared a good and gentle son. He spoke of her only on Mother's Day, when he would take my brother and me into the yard to find flowers for us to wear to church. We children each had a small red rose pinned to us, a sign that our mother was living. My father chose some white flower for himself, explaining that he wore white because his mother was dead. That's all. I wish now that I had been more curious and begged him to tell us about her. But I suspect that I was put off by the picture on his bureau, the same one that now adorns my desk. She just didn't look like a warm and cozy grandma.

I have given the glasses to my son. The pathetic little quilt top is tucked away at the back of the linen closet. But her picture stands on my desk. Maybe if I look at it long enough, I will come to know the silent peasant woman whose DNA I carry. I wonder what her voice was like. Did she sing at her work when she was alone in the house? Did her German bear the hearty accent of Swabia, or had it become corrupt and Americanized? Was she happy, or was she sad? For that

matter, did she permit herself the luxury of feelings?
Did she have choices, or was she the victim of harsh
circumstances?

My silent, stolid German grandmother has become
emblematic for me of all the silent women. Just as I
know so little of her story because there are no words,
I know so little of my foremothers in Scripture—
because there are no words.

I would love to hear Sarah's version of the almost-
sacrifice of Isaac. Or for that matter, what did she say
when Abram told her that the Lord was sending them
on a wild goose chase, away from Haran and all that
they knew and valued? And Lot's daughters—I would
love to know their version of the events at Sodom. We
move so lightly over the terrible ending of that story,
where their father pleads with the mob at the door: "I
beg you, my brothers, do not act so wickedly. Look, I
have two daughters who have not known a man; let me
bring them out to you, and do to them as you please;
only do nothing to these men, for they have come
under the shelter of my roof" (Genesis 19:7–8). What
words did Jephthah's daughter use to "bewail her vir-
ginity" in the two months granted her before her
pointless death at her father's hand? (Judges 11: 30–40).
Perhaps she had no words, but only inarticulate weep-
ing.

But it is the prophet Anna who reminds me most of
my silent grandmother, maybe because she too was a
widow and should have been a grandmother. We all
know the story: when the infant Jesus was presented in
the temple, the aged and devout Simeon recognized
the child as the Messiah. We have his words in the *Nunc
dimittis,* embedded in our prayer book in the liturgies

of Evening Prayer and Compline. Anna was also present, named by Luke as a prophet.

> She was of great age, having lived with her husband seven years after her marriage, then as a widow to the age of eighty-four. She never left the temple but worshiped there with fasting and prayer night and day. At that moment she came, and began to praise God and to speak about the child to all who were looking for the redemption of Jerusalem. (Luke 2:36b–38)

What did she say, this old, old prophet woman? She never left the temple, but prayed there night and day. My German grandmother never left the farmhouse, but labored there night and day. What did she say, this old, wordless peasant woman?

In Defense of a Woman
Named Martha

> Now as they went on their way, Jesus entered
> a certain village, where a woman named Martha
> welcomed him into her home.
>
> *(Luke 10:38)*

These days I'm pretty much a Mary. With children grown, household simplified, and days of business entertaining a distant memory, I am increasingly free to sit at the Lord's feet and listen to what he is saying. Not that I slow down and do so; like most of us, I am adept at avoidance and easily distracted. But my obligatory Martha-days are over.

I must confess that I read this story from Luke's gospel in an argumentative spirit. Jesus' pedagogical intent is clear: in the grand scheme of things, there is need of only one thing, and Mary has indeed chosen the better part. But where, I ask, would he be without Martha? And why, I ask crabbily, did he seek her hospitality if he then intended to belittle her? Why didn't he just stay out by the roadside for his teaching, if that was all that mattered?

My irritation grew when I read the footnote supplied in my New Oxford Annotated Bible (NRSV):

> With delicate ambiguity Jesus rebuked Martha's choice of values; a simple meal (one dish) is sufficient for hospitality. Jesus approved Mary's preference for listening to his teaching. . . as contrasted with Martha's unneeded acts of hospitality.

This is a relatively typical interpretation, polarizing the sisters and putting poor Martha ever more in the wrong. She lives in our minds as the ultimate Pelagian, the ultimate co-dependent, the ultimate fussy hostess. I think it's time to reclaim her!

Martha was the householder. She was in charge; she welcomed Jesus into *her* home. Did Jesus know what went into her preparations for his visits? What did he know about housework in general? He turned water into wine, effortlessly, at the last minute when supplies ran out at the wedding feast. He fed thousands, again seemingly without effort, somehow turning a little bread and two fish into abundance. But did he really understand Martha-work?

Martha-work is invisible when it is done right. The rooms are orderly, the clothes are clean, the food is good and plentiful; and it all seems just to *happen*. Martha's mistake perhaps was that she tried too hard and that—like most of us—she grew tired of being invisible. Maybe she got tired of never sitting down to enjoy her own parties. Maybe she got tired of being the careful older sister, the woman of the house, the one responsible for everyone else's well-being and comfort.

I know that I have never achieved the true mind of a scholar because I cannot help taking sides. And I emphatically take sides in this story! When I imagine that comfortable house in Bethany—the smell of good things cooking, a clean, inviting room, maybe some flowers or fruit in a simple bowl, perhaps soft lamplight or sun streaming in a window, the gentle movement of air and the rustle of trees outside—I also visualize the kitchen. Admittedly, it's not a first-century Palestinian kitchen, but something out of middle-class, Midwestern life in the 1930s. It's hot, the workspace is inadequate, all the dishtowels are soggy, the dishwater's getting cold, and the dirty pots and pans are piling up. And poor Martha, distracted by her many tasks, has just about had it.

Martha is giving Jesus her best. I suspect that she is constitutionally unable to drop everything and sit at his feet. Maybe later, after dinner, and after the dishes are done, but certainly not until she has offered him her hospitality. We rely on the Marthas to get the job done and to postpone their own pleasures until all obligations are met. To be sure, it's easy for a Martha to get carried away, not by selfish diversions, but by her own expanding vision of her work. So she probably was distracted by her many tasks and possibly so caught up in the minutiae of hospitality that she missed the point of welcoming Jesus into her home. But I think she deserves a gentle welcome to her own living room, not a reproach.

Another confession: I'm afraid I suspect Mary of being spoiled. I'm convinced that *her* fingernails weren't broken and *her* hands weren't rough from doing the laundry. That's the cranky, self-righteous Martha in me coming out. If I were Martha, my complaint to Jesus would be less restrained: "Don't you care that I've been left with all the work that no one wants to do? Don't you think that I might like to sit at your feet, but there's still dinner to prepare and a hundred small tasks to do. No one will notice that I do them, but they'll certainly notice if I neglect them. Have you ever wondered why you like to come to this house and not to the house next door or across the street when you are tired and hungry and when you yearn for a quiet space around you?"

Of course, I don't know how Jesus said, "Martha, Martha." Maybe he touched her gently on the arm or took her hand. Maybe he smiled the kind of loving smile that made her understand instantly. Speaking as a woman, though, I think he was risking a lot when he compared her to her sister. I doubt very much that she wanted to hear about Mary's spiritual giftedness.

Martha is the practical sister. In John's story of the raising of Lazarus, she makes a profound theological statement in confessing Jesus as the Christ and then— very much the woman with both feet on the ground— warns that the resurrected Lazarus will stink after four days in the grave. Martha is tough; Martha is real.

The people of the High Middle Ages knew this. Meister Eckhart preached on her spiritual maturity, indeed her superiority to her sister. "Martha knew Mary," he says, "better than Mary knew Martha." I think he was right: the Marthas see what is going on, even when their own presence is scarcely noted.

We need to reclaim Martha, honor her, maybe even thank her for the order and comfort she brings to our lives. Most of the time I would rather be Mary, or at least I think I would. I much prefer study to house-cleaning. Presence at the liturgy surely brings me closer to God than time spent mopping the kitchen floor. Time given to prayer feels richer than time endured in committee meetings.

On the other hand, maybe I am still a Martha, even though I no longer put everything aside to care for a child or prepare a big dinner. Maybe I want to go on being Martha, so long as I can reserve the right for occasional affectionate complaint: "Lord, do you not care that my sisters and brothers have left me to do all the work by myself? Tell them then to help me."

Spiritual Life in Cyberspace

L eni Pfeiffer, the eccentric protagonist in Nobel
prizewinner Heinrich Böll's novel *Group Portrait
with Lady,* experienced visitations from the Blessed
Virgin Mary when she sat alone before her empty television screen. It's a long time since I read the book,
and now I can't remember whether she ever figured
out that the vision was really her own dim reflection in
the darkened glass.

I sometimes find myself thinking about the fictional
Leni Pfeiffer as I sit before my computer monitor. I
can't claim mystical experiences—at least up to now—
but the spiritual fallout from the Internet has taken me
by surprise. For a long time I had resisted going on-
line, perfectly satisfied to use my elegant IBM as a kind
of glorified typewriter and filing system. Finally,
though, my computer maven persuaded me to get con-
nected, if only to have access to technical assistance.
With her help, I settled on an e-mail address and chose
a server. I couldn't imagine using either, decidedly not
with any pleasure, but permitted myself a certain smug
satisfaction in my up-to-dateness.

Much of my resistance arose from the fear that I
would be required to use some trendy new jargon,
indeed find a whole new way of communicating. At
the local mega-bookstore I got one of those bulky
paperbacks designed to reassure the inept (sometimes

referred to as dummies). My resistance increased expo-
nentially as I read of all sorts of arcane abbreviations
and cute symbols to bypass words. I felt as if I were wit-
nessing, if not participating, in the destruction of the
language of Shakespeare and the *Book of Common
Prayer.* "I'll never get it," I told myself, "and I'm not
even sure that I want to."

I don't know precisely when I succumbed to the
enchantment of e-mail. I suspect that it came upon me
gradually, but now I know that I am hooked. Like Leni,
I sit expectantly before the screen—not awaiting a
prophetic manifestation of the BVM, but enjoying a
lively sense of connection with friends around the
globe.

To be sure, e-mail is dangerous when the message is
thoughtless, angry, or hurtful. Emily Dickinson was
right on the money when she wrote:

> A word is dead
> When it is said,
> Some say.
> I say it just
> Begins to live
> That day.*

Once you click on "Send," those very alive words are
gone, out of your control, never to be recalled. So far
I've not been tempted to electronic indiscretion or the
venting of unbridled rage since most of my e-corre-
spondence is with good friends. To send them a spontaneous message is like sending a loving thought. I can
postpone writing "real" letters almost forever. Spoiled
child of my time that I am, it seems like so much work
to address an envelope, find a stamp, and walk three
minutes to the mailbox. And as for casual telephone

---

* *The Complete Poems of Emily Dickinson*, ed. Thomas H. Johnson (Boston: Little
Brown and Company, 1960), 534–535.

calls: will I interrupt a meal or wake someone up? Or, more than likely, will I simply start a round of telephone tag as machine talks to machine?

I pray that I will never take for granted the ease of communication with my spiritual friends scattered around the world. There is Janet in England, who has been my spiritual sister for twenty years. We pick up the phone occasionally, but both of us are sufficiently conservative to be a little awed by transoceanic calls "just to talk." But a casual, e-greeting is something else! There is Sue in Sydney. We were together for only a weekend, but quickly recognized our spiritual kinship. It seems only right to inquire from time to time about the well-being of her aging cat Spike. Just typing in her address brings back memories of a shared time that was holy. Brothers Andrew and Timothy, dear old friends in their monastery high on a ridge in the East Cape region of South Africa—what a joy to write to them with no agenda, just to remind them and myself of our unbroken connectedness, despite the thousands of miles between us. In some cases, I write to friends whom I have never seen. I will meet Ekman for the first time when I go to Hong Kong next year, but in the meantime our cordiality grows with each message exchanged.

I have learned also that the Internet can be a path to intercession. Twice in the past year, I have been part of a great web of intercessors, praying for the recovery of accident victims. One was the child of old friends, the other a man whom I had met only once at a conference. Updates would go out almost daily, my e-mail address tucked in among dozens of others. Sometimes there would be a message: call Michael and Carol; even if they are not home, they will be heartened by a voice

on the machine. Sometimes an address: don't visit, but
send a card. I knew very few people who were part of
those circles, but we were united in our prayerful
intention, part of a great web of friendship.

Two days before Christmas I found myself baking
Stollen, a sweet German bread that has long been part
of our family's holiday tradition. When I checked my
e-mail that evening, there was a greeting from Patricia,
my spiritual friend in Buenos Aires. We have met face-
to-face only once, but we have an ongoing lively conversation on the Internet. I had told her about my
afternoon of using my hands, lovely smells of sweet
dough rising, and the sense of Christmas that holiday
baking evoked. Her almost instantaneous reply: "I
know what you mean. I've been making *Pannetone*
today." Two hemispheres apart, two very different ethnic traditions—and we could have been in the same
room.

Those big frightening paperbacks of instruction for
dummies have really missed the point.

The Canaanite Woman

The story of the Canaanite woman (Matthew 15:21–28) is a hard gospel. It is almost an embarrassment because Jesus doesn't behave as I expect him to, as I think he should. Most assuredly, it does not fit into my childhood picture of a gentle Jesus, meek and mild. He tries to ignore the desperate woman, who cries out for his mercy and help. The disciples back him up: "Send her away. She's a nuisance." The implication, of course, is that they have important work to do and that this troublemaker is impeding them.

The disciples are exemplary insiders, those whom decades ago the sociologist David Riesman, author of *The Lonely Crowd,* would call "inside dopesters." They are the people who matter, the ones who know what is going on. In a patriarchal society, they are male. They share the linguistic, ethnic, cultural, and religious background of their leader. They have been individually chosen by Jesus to make up his intimate group of followers. They are an inside group, if ever there was one.

The Canaanite woman, on the other hand, is so far outside that she is scarcely worthy of consideration as a human being. As a woman, she breaks all taboos by addressing an unknown male. As a Canaanite, she is not just a foreigner but unclean, dangerously contaminating in her otherness.

Yet she comes, unbidden and persistent; and, driven by her need, she tries to break into the group where she knows she is unwanted. She accepts the limitations imposed by her society. After all, she has no twenty-first-century ideas of democracy or women's liberation or even of her own human worth. She wants only what might be given to the dogs—wild, dirty, scavenging animals.

So she comes and makes a nuisance of herself, and by sheer persistence she gets what she so desperately wants—healing for her child. The woman and mother in me is drawn into her pain and desperation, and I find myself angry and puzzled that she must beg for her child's wholeness. It seems to be a very human, finite Jesus here, who lets himself be worn down by the doggedness of her faith—not the sophisticated faith of a theologian or the joyous faith of one who has witnessed a sign, but rather the primitive, almost animal trust of a mother protecting her child.

This faith touches him, gets to him, and he says: "Woman, great is your faith! Let it be done for you as you wish." We have had the disquieting experience of watching Jesus change his mind. We have seen his awareness of his own identity and mission grow before our very eyes.

Who is the Canaanite woman now? Whom have we placed outside our strictly drawn, although sometimes invisible lines? We see ourselves as welcome at the table, the beloved children at the family meal. Whom do we try to send away as unfit, unclean, unhuman, as less than the mangy dog who gobbles up scraps of garbage?

History has given us lots of answers to that question. The National Socialists persuaded themselves that their

Jewish brothers and sisters were less than human, hence fit for cruelty and extermination. Slave owners in our own country wrote solemn treatises about the black person's insensitivity to the heat of the sun and the pain of the lash.

But that's the past. Nazi Germany is a comfortable distance away, at least for most of us. We have never owned a slave, and I doubt that we have met any Canaanite women. Yet the question is still alive for us, in this time and in this place.

I know that I do not need to search my own conscience very deeply before I discover that, in my selfish eagerness to draw comfortable lines around myself, I have dismissed individuals and groups from inclusion at the table by seeing them as other, outside, and not quite human. Worst of all, I rarely do this with malice or even enthusiasm. Like the disciples, I am preoccupied and impatient at being intruded upon, and so I say, "Send her away, for she keeps shouting after us." I am too busy. My own carefully constructed identity is too absorbing. It is so good being an insider that there is no time or space for the outsider, the other.

This is a hard gospel. I have to confess that it is one of my least favorite, although I am drawn to it again and again. It doesn't say nice, warm, sentimental things about the human family. It makes me look carefully at myself and at others.

In it I can see myself, the lines I have drawn and the walls I have erected. And I am forced to see the other, all those whom I have placed outside those barriers. These are not often the scrubbed and beautiful people who are Madison Avenue's idea of the human family. They are children of the Third World, their bellies swollen with hunger and their minds dulled from years

of malnutrition. They are the emotionally and spiritually starved children of the poverty that exists in the
midst of our abundance. They are the caged men in
overcrowded prisons, men so filled with rage and
despair that they can no longer function within the
structure of our society. I grow defensive and angry
when I see people who mistrust me or even hate me
because I am the wrong age or sex or color.

When we let ourselves look, when we relinquish
our privileged insider status, we will see people who
puzzle us and maybe frighten us. We will see our own
time's equivalent of the Canaanite woman.

I have to remind myself that if I am attentive to
what I see, I will not find myself diminished or my
identity destroyed. I will still be one of the insiders, one
of the beloved children at the table. And the host at the
table is still our father. The implications of these two
little words—our father—are tremendous.

They allow no lines to be drawn, no exclusion. No
one who cries, "Have mercy on me" must be sent away.
There is no place for dogs under the table, but only
places for the children at the banquet. All the children,
our sisters and brothers.

Holy Agnosticism

What do you believe happens after death?" Not long ago a relative stranger asked me this question. It came out of the blue, rather like those times when your children ask you probing questions in loud voices and in public places. Maybe she asked it because my white hair put me predictably close to the second Great Threshold. Maybe she thought that, as clergy, I had some inside trader information. Maybe she was just making conversation, but I suspect that she really wanted some assurance that she was on the right path.

Almost reflexively, I replied, "I don't know, and I'm not sure I really care." The woman who had asked the question was disturbed, indeed angry at me. My response had sounded flip, I fear, as if I weren't taking the Last Things—Heaven, Hell, Death, and Judgment—seriously enough.

On reflection, I know that I had answered her truthfully: I don't know. None of us knows. Paul tells us that we see in a glass darkly, in a dim mirror. We have glimpses of God—all of them true, but all of them partial. We can journey beyond death only in our imaginations and in anticipation.

I am grateful that I have grown beyond the imaginings of my childhood. Then I envisioned eternity as an endless Midwestern Sunday afternoon, where you sat around in your scratchy, uncomfortable good clothes while angels played harps. Nothing to do. Certainly no active games and precious little laughter. A beautiful but boring landscape, or maybe cloudscape. Life after death—if you could call that life—was to be postponed for as long as possible.

Nowadays my imaginings are livelier. Maybe life after death will be a feast for the mind, like great expanses of time in the main reading room in the Library of Congress, only with good lighting and comfortable chairs. I will read all the books I haven't had time for up to now, and I will revisit old favorites.

Maybe that new life will be bountiful, like the homecoming picnics at the Martin City Methodist Church, where my father worshiped as a boy. These were joyful reunions of people who hadn't seen each other for years, maybe decades. Long tables in the churchyard were filled with an amazing array, an abundance possible only among people who knew nothing of calories, cholesterol, and fast food. Those afternoons seemed endless, but unlike the constrained inactivity of my childhood, they were filled with gentle movement, talk, and laughter as old friends moved about under the big elms, meeting and parting and meeting again.

Sometimes I yearn for reunions. Will my father, who died when I was twenty-four, be pleased at how I turned out? I know that he will be surprised, but will he be pleased? I play with the idea that I will see my grandfather whom I loved deeply and who died when I was nine. His was the first death in my young life, so that makes him my oldest personal acquaintance in the great cloud of witnesses. I'd love to talk with my mother, really talk as two old ladies together. We could speak the deep truths that eluded us in our forty-some years together. Maybe she would tell me about the dreams that had died years before my birth. She cooked and cleaned, but what did she really want? She was so pretty in her high school pictures, soft and just a little bit plump. Maybe she would tell me what happened to that hopeful-looking girl, a smart girl who could read Latin and was the first in our family to go to college. I would like to meet my German grandparents for the first time. If heaven is like Jerusalem on the day of Pentecost, we'll have no language problems, but in all events my German is serviceable. They could tell me the stories that my father had forgotten or, more likely in his zeal to be a good American, tried to forget. I wonder about my two lost babies, their lives stopped before anyone but their mother could think of them as anything but an amorphous "product of conception."

Martin Luther was sure that he would be united with his dog in the next life. "And thou, little doggie, shalt have a golden tail," he promised his faithful friend. Maybe my dogs will be around—the asthmatic fox terrier Peggy (quite by coincidence we shared a name), Daisy the spitz who was on the sidewalk waiting every day when I came home from school, along with my assorted neurotic dachshunds. I'm not so sure about the cats. They never found their way into Holy Scripture, and they may be too arrogant and willful to find their way into heaven.

Will Dorsha, my poet friend who died at ninety-three, be waiting for me as she promised? I loved her for her boldness in facing death, for her artist's curiosity about the new experience that awaited her on the other side. And after I've caught up with family and old friends, there are all the great souls whose lively words have filled my bookshelves. Maybe there will be a corner where I can have a beer with Meister Eckhart, or some rocking chairs where I can crochet and chat with Dame Julian while she sews on humble garments, suitable for anchorites. Teresa of Avila would probably be tolerant of my halting Spanish, but I'm not sure that Thérèse of Lisieux and I would have much in common. I think I'll be more at home with the earthier saints.

I love to let my imagination run loose, but ultimately, I don't care. I don't care because at a deep level I believe Jesus' promise in John's gospel. He assures us that there are many rooms in his father's house (14:1–3). I don't need to know the floor plan and decor. It is enough that he has promised that he will come and take me to himself. At seventy-three, I have now lived most of my life, at least this part of it, and I believe with my wise fourteenth-century friend Julian of Norwich that it will ultimately be all right. I'm in no hurry, but when the time comes, it will be one more journey to a new place. There will be a room for me, and it will be a bountiful homecoming.

Words

word: something that is said...a speech sound or series of speech sounds that symbolizes and communicates a meaning without being divisible into smaller units capable of independent use...a written or printed character or combination of characters representing a spoken word....

word: *[Often cap.]* Logos, the divine wisdom manifest in the creation, government, and redemption of the world and often identified with the second person of the Trinity.★

★ *Merriam-Webster's Collegiate Dictionary,* tenth edition (Springfield, MA: Merriam-Webster, 1993).

Learning to Read

Last night around ten o'clock my son called. We normally don't talk this late, unless there is a real emergency: households with very young and seriously aging people are respectful of bedtimes. John knew that his father would already be asleep, but he was equally sure that I would be reading or—more likely, since it was Wednesday—watching *Law and Order*. (I'm not addicted to violent cop shows, but this particular series gives me a quick fix of the gritty city that I have loved and left.)

"Hi, Ma, I had to tell you what Jack just did." Jack is my almost-six grandchild, one more introvert in a long line of introverts. He's handsome, athletically gifted, and overall brilliant, as of course all grandchildren are. "He was supposed to be asleep, but he just turned up in the living room, plunked himself down on the sofa, and read us one of his Little Bear books from cover to cover. Then he told us, 'This is what I do in my spare time' and went back to bed."

My son and I talked for a bit about the joy of reading, how glorious to discover it as a gift instead of struggling laboriously to conquer it as an enemy. After our conversation, I found that I had lost interest in the pursuit of justice on the city streets. Instead, I was remembering the day I learned to read.

I was about Jack's age. Unlike him, I didn't possess a whole cupboard full of beautifully illustrated, thoughtfully written books. Also unlike him, I didn't live in a neighborhood with a library, let alone a library with a well-stocked children's room. But from my earliest memory I had been talked to and read to. My happiest hours were sharing my grandfather's big rocking chair, where he read me the same stories over and over and—when we had exhausted the meager supply of children's books—the latest news in the *Kansas City Star.*

I learned to read on a bright winter day. I was alone in the little room off the dining room. For some reason, it was called "the den," which suggests a cozy study or retreat of some sort. Actually, no one ever retreated there, except my grandmother to use her old treadle Singer sewing machine and I to find a quiet corner. I was sitting on the floor looking at one of my big brother's old Bobbs-Merrill readers. These were dreary little books, sparsely illustrated with beige-gray pictures. I can still feel my shock, an epiphany really, when the words suddenly made sense. The story was not much more interesting than the pictures that accompanied it, but my excitement lay in the thrill of decoding the little groups of letters. (Like young Jack, it seemed as if I had known the letters forever, but just didn't know what to do with them.)

The first story I read on that winter day was the moralistic fable of the little red hen. I won't recount it here, but it presented a cynical picture of human selfishness and unhelpfulness. It was at the same time a paean to the work ethic: the little red hen came out on top because she managed to do the work all by herself, thank you very much!

From that first day there has been no turning back. The wonder has never diminished. The magic of words, words all by themselves and words strung together to make poetry and stories and encyclopedias—if anything, that magic has increased. I love the words knit together by others, and I love words that I knit together—in conversations, in teaching, in writing. Playing with words is holy play.

But young Jack and I are missing a lot if we stay at the level of Little Bear and his high-achieving chicken ancestor. We're missing a lot even if we stay with Shakespeare and Goethe and Plato. The Word is more than letters strung together, and learning to read is more than an exercise in decoding printed symbols.

Each Christmas Eve we hear the mysterious, provocative prologue to John's gospel: "In the beginning was the Word, and the Word was with God, and the Word was God. . . . And the Word became flesh and lived among us" (John 1:1, 14a).

This is not a Word to be found in the graded readers of my childhood or in the "I Can Read" series that is introducing young Jack to the delights of the printed page. It's certainly never found in whatever contrived bad writing has now replaced poor old Dick and Jane of the fifties, sixties, and seventies. This Word isn't even in the *Oxford English Dictionary.*

In one of his Christmas sermons, Meister Eckhart says that God speaks his eternal Word in the soul and thus is born in that soul.* To read this Word, to know this Word, and to be embraced by this Word is the work of a lifetime. And then some.

I'm just beginning to learn to read.

---

* *Dum medium silentium,* sermon 57 in *DeutschePredigten und Traktate,* ed. Josef Quint.

Words

One of my favorite icons is propped in a bookcase at eye-level beside my rocking chair. It's a reproduction of an ancient fresco from a Greek church. A benign and slightly flabby Adam, sitting on a large rock, is naming the animals. They stand before him in a delightful array. Unlike the later procession boarding the ark, one of each is sufficient. There is a benevolent-looking snake, a slightly petulant lion, a peacock, an inattentive rabbit, and a griffin—to name just a few. God is nowhere in the picture. Adam is on his own.

I love this icon for its gentleness. The animals—all of whom look like vegetarians—are getting along nicely, and Adam seems aware of the responsibility entrusted to him when the Lord God gave him dominion over all the flying, creeping, swimming, and prancing creatures. It's a quaint little picture of Eden before the Fall.

I love this picture even more for what it says about our humanity: Adam is *naming* the animals. These are his first words. I wonder whether they came easily, or whether he had to study each creature for a long, long time and then perhaps struggle with his lips and tongue and teeth before the vowels and consonants came together in his mind and in his mouth. Was he surprised at this new gift of forming words? Did he maybe laugh now and then when he came up with a particularly good name? Did he alternate long ones and short ones, just to keep from getting bored?

And did he remember all the names after he had bestowed them? After all, the gift of memory is inextricably linked with God's gift of language.

When I was a little girl, I liked the sound of words even when I didn't understand them. I liked long words because they were especially filled with mystery. I recall learning the Our Father when I was very small, certainly no more than three. My favorite word was "temptation," pronounced by me to a slightly syncopated beat as "temp-a-*ta*-shun." I hadn't a clue what it meant, but I enjoyed the feel of its syllables in my mouth.

I liked the German words my father told me when we were in the garden together. They were special, with very different sounds from our everyday Midwestern English. They gave me a glimpse into another world, one that looked precisely like the one I inhabited but where familiar sights and sounds and thoughts all had different names.

When I was a little older, maybe eight or nine, someone told me about Pig Latin, *ig-pay, atin-lay*, that is. I wonder: are children still discovering the fun of rearranging syllables so that the words sound like another language? I quickly became a fluent speaker of Pig Latin, sure that I had unlocked a great mystery. I was profoundly disappointed when some well-meaning adult told me that it wasn't a real language at all.

My next linguistic adventure came in the ninth grade when I enrolled in "real" Latin. As a teacher, I look back at my memories of that class and am tempted to weep. Had I not been in hot pursuit of that nameless Something that had haunted me all my young life, I would have found it boring. We plodded through a watered-down Caesar, with no sense at all of what he was doing in Gaul—to say nothing of what or where Gaul was. It was not enough to translate stilted sentences from Latin to English; we labored at translating English to Latin, a skill useful only to those planning to work in the Vatican. (An unlikely future for anyone in our staunchly Protestant community.)

Things lightened up occasionally when we learned Latin translations of familiar songs. I can still sing—in Latin—"Jingle Bells," "Row, Row, Row Your Boat," and "Twinkle, Twinkle, Little Star" as well as recite the Pledge of Allegiance—at least up to a point. Now and then Miss Smith enlivened our usual slogging pace with a rapid oral drill on demonstrative pronouns. Going around the room, up and down the aisles we would recite *hic, haec, hoc,* [pause for breath] *huius, huius, huius,* [pause again] *huic, huic, huic,* [pause] *honc, hanc, hoc,* [pause] *hoc, hac hoc* [enormous sigh of relief]. Adam surely had more fun naming the animals, but at least it was a change of pace. I enjoyed it, even though I found it meaningless, but for those merely enduring the class it must have been a minor torture.

Miss Smith's Latin class was a beginning, merely a taste. She went off and joined the WAVES so I didn't experience the wonders of the second-year course until much later when I was in college. (In retrospect I realize that Miss Smith probably wasn't enjoying the class much, either. Military service must have been a welcome relief.)

Tedious as it had been and quite divorced from meaning, that Latin class had given me a glimpse of the mystery of language. I wanted more! My college required two years of a foreign language. "Take

German," my father said, "it's easy." It wasn't, but at last I could fling myself into my love affair with words ancient and modern, known and unknown, pronounceable and unpronounceable. Over the years I've dabbled in more Latin, some French, a taste of Old Icelandic (along with other obscure Germanic languages), and a bit of Swedish. I can manage housewife Spanish well, if inelegantly. I love sliding back and forth from English to German, although this doesn't come so easily now as it used to. I marvel at the subtle changes in me and in my perceptions when I approach the familiar with new sounds. The landscape of the Psalms read in Spanish seems very different from the still waters and green pastures of the *Book of Common Prayer.* The *Vater unser* has a different flavor from the Our Father of my childhood—a little more serious, maybe, but equally reassuring.

Rilke, writing to the now forgotten young poet, adjured him to love the questions, to love them like books written in a very strange language.

> Be patient toward all that is unsolved in your heart and try to love the questions themselves like locked rooms and books that are written in a very foreign tongue. Do not seek to know the answers, which cannot be given you because you would not be able to live them. And the point is, to live everything. Live the questions now.★

I still love the words, and I'm growing into loving the questions. Even when I don't know the answers. Yet.

★ Rainer Maria Rilke, *Letters to a Young Poet,* trans. M. D. Herter Norton (New York: W. W. Norton, 1962), 35.

So — *What Was the Question?*

Human beings are born questioners. The interrogative is the grammatical mood favored by the very young. Parental delight in the first words uttered by the toddler begins to wear thin as the flood of questions swells. One "Why?" leads inexorably to another with no end in sight. As speech develops, the questions become probing and specific, and the typical articulate four-year-old is an uninhibited and persistent master of interrogation. Why is that lady so fat? Why does that man have only one arm? How does the baby get inside the mother's tummy? Who was the first person *ever*? Who was his mother? Will you die some day? What happens when you die?

Relatively early, we are socialized out of asking questions, at least questions that really matter. We become discreet; we learn subtlety and indirection. At the same time, we learn to be cautious about the questions of others. Will I give the right answer? That is, will my answer guarantee a good grade and enable me to pass the course? Or will I reveal my deficiencies? Will my answer lead to reward or punishment? Most threatening of all, will I reveal myself?

In his humanity, Jesus asked questions too. His first recorded words are a question to his anxious mother: "Why were you searching for me? Did you not know that I must be in my Father's house?" (Luke 2:49). And his last anguished cry from the cross was also a question: "My God, my God, why have you forsaken me?" (Matthew 27:46).

He never got out of the habit of asking direct, probing questions. "Whom do you seek? What do you want? What do you want me to do for you? How many loaves have you? Who do people say that I am? Do you know what I [as I kneel to wash your feet] have done to you? Why are you sleeping?" His questions always demanded an answer, and he was willing to wait for it. His questions bear no resemblance to the multiple-choice queries of standardized tests, nor are they easy examples of the true-false variety. They get at the truth. They force us to see ourselves and know ourselves. They press us to articulate what we truly want. They are never trivial conversation. Jesus asks questions that challenge, open new vistas, and lead us to the next step.

In John's account of the breakfast on the shore (John 21), Jesus asks his final question, the most important one of all. Calling Peter by name, he asks, "Do you love me?" Not once, but three times. He asks it of Peter, who had protested, "Lord, why can I not follow you now? I will lay down my life for you" (John 13:37). Of Peter, who had cowered in the courtyard denying everything. Of Peter, whose treachery was more wounding than that of Judas because Peter—like most of us—embodied that unholy muddle of love and betrayal.

It is immensely satisfying to be able to distinguish the good guys from the bad guys, to identify the villains and consign them to damnation. It is harder to live with the reality that, like Peter, we are unable to live up to our intentions. Like his, our love and commitment are genuine. It is easy to imagine the joy with which he jumped into the sea, too impatient to wait for the heavily laden boat to travel the hundred yards to the shore where Jesus was waiting. Yet his joy had to be tinged with shame and guilt: how could he face the Teacher whom he had denied? That's something in Peter I can identify with. Something in us—call it weakness, call it our human fallenness, call it sin—can lead us to betrayal even when we are desperate to love.

Jesus' question to Peter lies at the heart of their relationship. He asks it with love, but he is unrelenting and tough. Each repetition inevitably and painfully recalls a denial of that relationship. Yet it is hardly an inquisition, but rather a final shared meal. How, I wonder, can we remember the Last Supper so vividly and enshrine it liturgically, yet somehow neglect the powerful message of the breakfast picnic? It is a homey scene, with Jesus presiding as cook and host. "[He] came and took the bread and gave it to them, and so with the fish." And then he institutes the Sacrament of the Second Chance: "Do you love me? Do you love me? Do you love me?"

There is no question of *his* love; it has never been in question. Amazingly, while he bears the physical wounds of the crucifixion, there has been no breach or rupture in his love for the most fallible of his friends. Our experience of human forgiveness is most often flawed. Even the most generous of us finds it hard to forget, and it is tempting to hold on to a bit of self-righteousness even as we declare that the broken relationship is restored and that everything is just as it was before. Similarly, it is hard to accept forgiveness, maybe even more difficult than to forgive. Shame lingers, even when restitution is made and guilt is expunged.

But at the breakfast on the shore, restoration is complete. Peter answers the questions and passes the test. But it is costly. Love is always costly. Perhaps that is why we fear it and betray it. Peter is given work to do: to feed and tend Christ's lambs and sheep. For years whenever I read this passage from the end of John's gospel, I would stop here, with warm thoughts about sheep and lambs. There is such balance and symmetry in it: the question, the protestation of love, and the command to loving service, all repeated three times. It's a neat and satisfying story.

But the story doesn't stop there. What follows is a reminder of the inevitability of loss that is a part of martyrdom, whether ours is the witness of those who face the fierce wild beast or the more ordinary, even humdrum faithfulness of those who simply go on putting one foot in front of the other. It is a reminder that at some point we will return to the helplessness and impotence of infancy: someone else will dress us and carry us where we do not wish to go. It is a reminder that freedom in Christ is ultimately powerlessness.

"Margaret, do you love me?"

"Lord, you know everything; you know that I love you." Will I, like Peter, be able to follow?

Small Words To Be Used With Care

When I was a child, there were a number of forbidden words—short, hard, little words that were four letters long. Nice children never said them or even heard them. Some of them were so forbidden that I didn't even know what they were, but I was sure that they were out there somewhere. Occasionally I saw them chalked on sidewalks, and once—horrors!—someone scratched a choice selection into the blackboard of the eighth-grade history room. (The perpetrator was never identified.) I was an adult before I ever heard most of them spoken. Over the years I have schooled myself to look nonchalant when they are uttered in my presence, for it is important that clergy appear unshaken when exposed to the language of the so-called real world. There are still those who view us as rarefied beings and apologize profusely at a slip of the tongue. I try to assure them that they haven't said anything I haven't heard before.

But I confess discomfort, when I hear those old forbidden words issuing from the mouths of babes or when an otherwise inoffensive movie is liberally sprinkled with old Anglo-Saxon expletives, just to achieve an R-rating and thereby assure a good box office. (In passing I would note my ethnic resentment at the Anglo-Saxon attribution: the traditionally forbidden words are part of our Germanic heritage, remnants of the less elegant ancestral branch of our hybrid English.)

At any rate, there are fewer and fewer words that cannot be uttered anywhere and by anyone. Even some little old ladies of my acquaintance have developed salty vocabularies. I lament the loss of forbidden words; the language is weaker without them—flatter and lacking its old potential for magic. So perhaps it's time to create a new list of dangerous words, not to replace the old Anglo-Saxon catalogue of body parts and functions, but to move the whole subject to a higher plane. Or to a place of greater depth.

There are plenty of four-letter words that should be treated with greater care, perhaps to be uttered less frequently and then with intent. *Work* needs be reclaimed and honored. It means much more than "task" or "job." Work can be holy. Work can be life-giving and life-changing. It can also become an obsession and consume us. It can be our false god, or it can be a path to God.

And then there is *rest*—how difficult it is! We work hard at recreation, forgetting that it is not the same as re-creation. True rest is restorative, providing the needed balance with work. Not the same as idleness, rest is commanded by the God who ordained the Sabbath; it is our ultimate goal. After all, Augustine reminds us that our souls are restless until they find their rest in God. Why else do we pray that the souls of the faithful departed may rest in peace? Rest, like work, can be holy.

Then there are fierce little hurtful words to be used with great caution. *Hate*—when I dare to hate something or someone, I want them to cease to be. I want them cast into outer darkness. I try to be careful with this word and am ashamed when it slips casually from my lips. The same is true for *kill,* with its dreadful finality. Every day the television offers me the doubtful pleasure of murderous voyeurism. Even if I refrain from taking life, even from swatting one of those pesky mosquitoes in the backyard, I can entertain myself by watching an astonishing variety of killings.

The big little word, maybe the one to be used with the greatest care, is none of the above. It is *love,* the most powerful of all the potent four-letter words, whether holy or obscene. Just as I try to be careful about casual use of *hate* and *kill* and *damn,* I am trying to be more thoughtful when I speak of *love.*

Love is hard—hard to understand and hard to live into. Jesus says to his friends, "I give you a new commandment, that you love one another" (John 13:34). This is absurd, if not impossible. In memory, I hear my grandmother's voice, enjoining my big brother and me to love one another, since God had given us to each other as brother and sister. We glared at each other and marveled at her naiveté. The very idea of loving somebody because we were *supposed* to boggled our childish minds. I suspect that the disciples felt much the same way.

And the idea is still mind-boggling, at least if we buy into the idea that love has anything to do with how we feel. We have cheapened love by our careless use of the word. We have confused the sentimentality of the Hallmark card with the deep, dark mystery of love manifested and embodied for us in the incarnate Christ. Yes, love can be warm, enfolding, and sheltering. Yes, love can feel good. But love can be also be strong, difficult, a fearsome challenge.

We need to be cautious when we talk about love.

Whatever Became of Sin?

O n my shelf is a crumbling paperback bearing this
title, bought nearly a quarter of a century ago for
$2.25. It is a wise book by psychiatrist Karl Menninger.
As I leaf through it—leafing through neglected old
friends on the top shelf of the bookcase is a pleasurable form of procrastination when I am avoiding *real*
work—I realize maybe for the first time how truly wise
it is. I wish that it had been required reading when I
was studying for the priesthood, and I wish that I had
had the good sense to assign it to my students.

Despite the inclusion of two forms of the Rite of
Reconciliation in the 1979 *Book of Common Prayer* and
despite regular if perfunctory recitation of the General
Confession in the liturgy, sin has fallen on hard times.
Most frequently these days I encounter references to it
in restaurant reviews: high calorie, high fat desserts—
almost always chocolate—are routinely described as
"sinful" or "sinfully delicious." This has become a grat-
ing cliché in the cliché-ridden purple prose of culinary
criticism. While I'm pretty sure that, for my physical if
not spiritual health, I should abstain from the desserts
described, I doubt that occasional indulgence would
rank very high on any scale of transgressions.

It's just not good form to talk about sin anymore.
Maybe it never was, at least not in polite society. I
learned this firsthand a few years ago when I submit-

ted an article for publication to one of the better-known journals of spirituality. I waited nearly a year for a response, then wrote to inquire about its fate. After much hemming and hawing, the editor said it was quite a good essay but that I would need to "soften it." "Soften what?" I asked, I who had spent decades trying to acquire sufficient toughness to say what I meant the first time. "Well," he replied, "in a couple of places you use the word 'sin' and once you describe certain behavior as 'wicked.' That will put people off, you know. Maybe you could say pretty much the same thing using other words." Simultaneously he rejected the article and I withdrew it. It wasn't *that* good anyway.

We didn't talk much about sin in my childhood, but awareness was in the air. In my genetic mix of German farmers and rock-ribbed New Englanders, a powerful inborn sense of right and wrong was part of the DNA. God, as I knew him then, was fair but unrelentingly tough. He—and *he* was very much the God of Michelangelo's ceiling—wasn't into second chances. So you had better get it right the first time. Fortunately for my spiritual comfort, I worked out my own categories that left a few moral loopholes. One never lied, but it was all right just not to tell everything you knew. One never hit, but one could devise more subtle methods of retaliation. (I could make my big brother carsick just by talking. I repent of this now—sort of.) Beyond that, one did not steal, murder, or commit adultery—whatever that was. Covetousness might have been tricky, except that everyone in our neighborhood was feeling the burden of the Depression, and we were slightly better off than our neighbors. So most of my friends did not have anything I really wanted.

Currently, when I comb through my conscience, I realize that most of my day-to-day sins aren't very interesting. They are tacky and shabby rather than exciting and flamboyant. In fact, they are downright boring—they will never make the stuff of movies. This doesn't, however, make them any less real or serious.

More impressive are those big sins that are recognized in retrospect. These are the sins that flourish untended in the rich soil of unawareness. The most powerful—and shaming—example in my memory goes back to my undergraduate years at the University of Kansas. This was well before any legislation that guaranteed the civil rights of African-American students to equal access to education. They were able to enroll in the university, but the dormitories remained segregated. Indeed, the idea that students with different skin colors would live under the same roof was scandalous. The YWCA offered the only racially integrated housing on campus, and it was regarded as highly suspect, possibly even Communist. The student union was closed on Sundays, and African-Americans were not served in the restaurants in town. I learned much later that they were fed by black families who took them in for Sunday dinner.

These were the children of taxpayers.

Reprehensible as these circumstances were, I can't excuse myself by claiming youth or political powerlessness. My sin was not noticing, not paying attention, and not asking questions. In the medieval courtly romance Parzival the naive young hero unwittingly perpetuates great suffering in the Grail community only because he does not ask a simple question: what's wrong? The question cries out to be asked but remains—for all the wrong reasons—unasked. In my unawareness and inattentiveness, I had not asked the question that cried out to be asked.

When I recall myself in those days of youthful comfort and complacency, I marvel: how could I have not noticed? How could I have not asked those simple, life-changing and life-giving questions? If I did not ask them aloud and publicly, how could I have avoided questioning myself?

That's an old sin. It's hard to atone for it after more than half a century, just as it is difficult for our country to atone for the horror of slavery. But when I am feeling brave, I must ask myself: what am I missing now? What am I carefully or carelessly not seeing? I suspect that I am still adept at willful unawareness.

There are questions that are still crying out to be asked.

A Secret Word

What can I say about Advent that hasn't been said already? Deploring pre-Christmas madness has become such a cliché that it's tempting to lapse into crankiness. After all, we began to hear "The Little Drummer Boy" in the supermarket almost before the old Halloween candy has been sold off at a reduced price. The catalogs have begun to flood our mailboxes. Harry and David are urging me to show my love with boxes of fruit while Lands' End suggests that gifts of clothing would be welcome. L.L. Bean promises to be a good resource if you're stuck on gift ideas for your dog. I haven't heard from Lillian Vernon lately—is she still around? In print and on television, we are deluged with advertisements urging us to hurry up and buy. Time is short; we're counting down the days.

Most of the time we don't think about it, but the brevity and the inexorable limitation of the weeks before Christmas are a reminder of the brevity and the inexorable limitation of our earthly life. Maybe it's a necessary exercise, even for those who profess no faith and little curiosity about the Last Things—a kind of fire drill, a relatively painless practice that bears minimal resemblance to the Real Thing.

I confess an addiction to those magazines by the supermarket checkout, not the lurid ones that tell of Elvis sightings and three-headed farm animals, but the wholesome ones that exhort me to bake cookies for a family that is on a permanent sugar and fat alert and to make a few more decorations for a house that is already full of dust catchers. Every November I tell myself, "You don't need that; you're grumpy enough already." But then I pay my $1.49 to read about winsome new ways of displaying Christmas cards on the mantel, enchanting centerpieces of Santas and reindeer, and—when I have reached the optimum level of frenetic activity—tips on how I can relax from the pressures of the season. My supermarket sources are big on a kind of generic meditation and soothing soaks in the tub, which seem to guarantee a quasi-mystical experience.

For Christians it is easy to be distracted, if not seduced by the sights and sounds of this season. Inundated by the superfluous and the superficial, we can lose sight of those awesome Four Last Things—Heaven, Hell, Death, and Judgment. It's more pleasant and certainly less demanding to plan how we'll drape the lights over the azaleas and where all the grandchildren will sleep when they come "home" for the holidays. Or where *we'll* sleep, if we're the traveling family members this year. It's certainly more pleasant to feel guilty that we haven't written *one single card* than to contemplate the eschaton. And most of us have no trouble filing those traditional, disturbing Advent gospel readings away somewhere in our subconscious to be considered later, when we have more time. Surely John the Baptist was talking about other well-meaning people of long-ago times and places when he tastelessly addressed his followers as a brood of vipers! I'm sure that it's good to hear those scary passages on Sunday morning, but there's no need to let them get to us.

But all of us, most assuredly the people whom the demographers designate as "senior," should probably begin to take life—and death—seriously. The repeated scriptural imperatives to watch and to wait—the very watchwords of the Advent season—are infinitely more serious than the light-hearted commands in the song we knew as children: "You better watch out, you better not cry, you better not pout, I'm telling you why: Santa Claus is coming to town!" We're watching and waiting, all right, but our watching and waiting bears little resemblance to listening for reindeer hoofbeats on the roof. Our faith demands that we live not only on the threshold, but perpetually on the alert, attentive to signs of his coming among us.

It's easy to get jaded—or depressed—when we have lived through quite a lot of Advents and especially when we are not in a ho-ho-ho mood. We can lament the seeming disappearance of Christ from the season. With chagrin I've noticed that in the past few years our zeal for inclusivity has reached the point where "Merry Christmas" is commonly replaced by the politically sensitive "Holiday Greetings." Advent calendars with chocolate behind the little windows are increasingly displacing the old-fashioned ones with little pictures that retell the old story of the Baby in Bethlehem.

But every year I discover anew that I am not nearly so grumpy as I thought. Every year I am surprised by the joy in this season of shorter days and growing darkness. Even as I resist holiday parties and never get around to sending Christmas cards (I *do* write a lot of Epiphany letters, though!), I can't help loving the season. I love the hymns and the awe-inspiring readings and collects. I rejoice to see blue and purple vestments and altar hangings after an interminable season of green. To my surprise, I've even come to love the very out-of-place "Little Drummer Boy" in the supermarket aisles and all the rest of the seasonal hype.

My growing tolerance is not the fruit of indifference or defeat, but rather my admiration of the impressive sneakiness of the God who chose to come among us as a baby. All babies are holy, even the funny-looking and fussy ones. But this baby is the Holy Child. What a great disguise! What a way of cutting through all pretentiousness and melting away complicated structures and hierarchies! What a way of getting people hooked, even when they aren't aware what has hooked them!

In his great hymn, Phillips Brooks prays, "Cast out our sin and enter in, be born in us today." Six hundred years earlier, my Dominican friend Meister Eckhart (who probably knew nothing about real, flesh-and-blood babies) said much the same thing when he preached compellingly that we should get ready for the birth of God in our soul. "In the midst of silence," he says, "a secret Word was declared to me."

So we get ready for the eternal newness of that birth. I wouldn't think of missing the children's service on Christmas Eve afternoon when our current parish baby—boy or girl—with beaming parents, and Willie, the slightly dilapidated papier-mâché donkey, make their way down the aisle. The reenactment of the old story is very dear, gentle, a little bit sentimental—but always new. It's not nearly so splendid as our midnight Eucharist, but it is a reminder of the simplicity and the immediacy, the wonder and the glory of his Advent. Once again, a secret Word has been declared to us.

Bridge Pipes

My holy place is a ramshackle old house in the Virginia Blue Ridge. More specifically, it sits on a dirt road in Jenkins Hollow. The Hazel River, fresh out of the Shenandoah Park, runs through the front yard, and the road is accessible by a low-water bridge.

This bridge is an unassuming concrete structure, with no railings, barely above the water. It has some broken edges and significant cracks. The river flows beneath it through five pipes. In the summer, snakes live in these pipes. They can grow to an impressive size, but are actually quite harmless—we are too far north for water moccasins. My snake book describes our river dwellers as "non-venomous, but irritable." Lethal-looking but probably quite harmless spiders spin their webs from the pipes to the surrounding rocks.

The river flows through the pipes smoothly in the summer. In the hot, dry season it might more correctly be termed a creek, transparent as it rattles over the stones. But everything changes with the autumn rains: then the water flows cold and deep, carrying a load of oak and sycamore leaves, plus assorted sticks great and small. Eventually, the flow is impeded and maybe stopped altogether when it reaches the bridge. The pipes become clogged, and the water rises over the bridge. Then it becomes difficult to cross, sometimes even impossible.

My ongoing challenge is to restore the flow through the blocked pipes. In the summer, standing in the cold water is a welcome exercise, but by November, it is much too cold to climb down into the river. Then the water is so swift and deep that, even standing on the bridge in my wellies, I can scarcely see what I am doing. Nevertheless, I arm myself with a sturdy stick or a hoe or a broom handle and go to work. This is a matter of strategic poking. Simply removing a clump of leaves that have turned to papier-mâché in the water or pulling out one little stick that has got crosswise across a pipe can release the flow. Then the force of the stream does the work: the cold mountain water gushes through the pipe, pushing before it little stones and trapped vegetation. The water level sinks dramatically, there is a rumbling and rattling as stuff moves through the pipes, and suddenly the bridge—like the Red Sea before the advancing Israelites—can be crossed with unmoistened foot.

I stand there clutching my stick or old broom handle, listening to the rush of water, and bask in a sense of accomplishment. Out of nowhere, I hear my father's voice, though he's been dead for nearly fifty years. I can hear him say gently, *"Honig, nicht mit Gewalt."* Honey, don't force it.

His first language was German. Unschooled, he acquired a quite elegant English by absorbing the King James Version of the Bible. But in my childhood, he sprinkled bits of German into his speech, especially when we were alone and he was not working so hard at being Anglicized. I was well into adolescence before I sorted out the German bits; they seemed so natural that, for a long time, I did not recognize them as "foreign." *"Nicht mit Gewalt,"* he would caution in the face of frustrating little tasks. "Don't force it"—whether I was wrestling impatiently with a recalcitrant jar lid or trying to turn a key in a resisting lock. In other words, don't use a big, violent gesture when a small, gentle one will do the trick.

He didn't know it then—or at least, I think that he didn't—but he was teaching me the unexpected power of small, decisive, healing gestures. He was teaching me that a thoughtful and gentle movement could accomplish more than an angry onslaught.

The little river in Jenkins Hollow is for me a picture of God. Or maybe a picture of God's love and grace, of God's peace flowing like a river. In hurricane season, it can be a picture of the terror of God. Or sometimes it is a picture of the soul's journey God-ward. Its symbolism shifts and changes, but it is always my teacher. And one of the questions it asks is this: where is the flow impeded? Where are we stuck? Where am I contributing to others' stuckness?

Of course, it's not a matter of poking myself or others with a stick. Rather, it's a matter of paying attention to little things and of recognizing when obstacles can be removed by the tiniest of gestures. The right word spoken at the right time can open the floodgates, letting hurts and resentments rattle harmlessly through the pipes, just as small stones are driven by the newly released, powerful flow. A graceful small yielding at the right moment can remove massive impediments—they just float away like the great masses of sycamore leaves. It doesn't take much—just the right touch in the right place. Sometimes you can't even see what you're doing as you balance precariously on the edge of the bridge. But it doesn't take much. *Nicht mit Gewalt!*

There Is So Much to Hear

I am remembering a piano recital I heard a half century ago at the Midwestern university where I was an undergraduate. It was a student recital, which meant that there was no admission charge. So it seemed an ideal Sunday afternoon break in my studies. The young pianist offered a program of predictable classics, adequately if not brilliantly played. It was, I realize now, a workmanlike performance, one hurdle to be jumped on the road to a degree from the music school. Yet given my naive fondness for almost all music, I had a wonderful time. I bathed myself in the notes and let them wash away all the ponderous words that I had been struggling with back in my dorm room. I admired the pianist—her poise, her ability to remember all those notes and then hit the right key, at least most of the time, and her overall artistic giftedness.

Then came the intermission. I was hovering around the edges of a group of fellow students, people with whom I'd shared classes, whom I knew but not very well. My pleasure in what I had just heard was swiftly marred by their vigorous dissection of the performance. Fingering, pedaling, phrasing, posture, stage presence, even the dress chosen for this more or less professional debut—nothing escaped their notice and belittling criticism. This was long before the word "deconstruction" entered our language, but the people

in our little circle didn't need a special word to explain
their cheerful absorption in demolition. They sounded
so sure! I was convinced that if they were offered a
place at the keyboard, they could do it better. I began
to be embarrassed that I was so naive as to have enjoyed
the concert up to this point and breathed a little prayer
of thanksgiving that I had said nothing to give my
enthusiasm away.

An old music professor had been standing at the
edge of the circle. He was a fixture on the campus, near
retirement, and picturesquely "foreign" in this school
surrounded by wheatfields. His Italianate name and his
Old World accent, which had lingered after decades in
the Middle West, made him an exotic figure in this part
of the country where German, Scandinavian, or New
England ancestry was the norm. He listened to the
increasingly intense—and petty—disparaging pronouncements. Then, when it was almost time to return
to our seats, he spoke: "But there is so much to hear!"

The circle fell silent. There was really nothing more
to say. He was right: even in a not-very-inspired performance, there was a lot to hear. Brahms and
Beethoven had refused to be overshadowed.

His words have stayed with me for over fifty years.
There is such a fine line between mindless acceptance
of anything that comes our way—whether it is food,
music, or the latest hit movie—and the urge to dissect.
It can be fun to distance ourselves from all sorts of
experiences by coolly identifying flaws and shortcom-
ings. Then to line them up neatly, rather like the time I
took my alarm clock apart, with not a clue how to
restore the bits and pieces to anything like working
order. I am sure that the professor, whose name I have
long forgotten, heard every imperfection. He could

have sat with that piano student and shown her many ways to improve her performance. I am equally sure that he would have done this lovingly, out of love for the student whose promise he recognized and even more out of love for the music itself.

It is good to have high standards of taste and achievement. God deserves our best efforts, and our best efforts deserve to be honored. There is great humility and simplicity in this offering of our best. There is also great wisdom in discriminating between the best and the second rate. A touch of humility and simplicity can be a great help here too. We can miss hearing the music if we let ourselves be distracted by small things. If we let ourselves become jaded or hyper-critical, we can lose the gift of joy and wonder that was prayed for at our baptism.

> Heavenly Father, we thank you that by water and the Holy Spirit you have bestowed upon these your servants the forgiveness of sin, and have raised them to the new life of grace. Sustain them, O Lord, in your Holy Spirit. Give them an inquiring and discerning heart, the courage to will and to persevere, a spirit to know and to love you, and the gift of joy and wonder in all your works. (*Book of Common Prayer*, 308)

It's a great prayer. I wish that it were repeated more frequently, prayed on behalf of all of us sophisticated folk of high standards and not just invoking this great gift for the new Christian. In my parish, most of our baptisands are babies and young children. They haven't lost the gift of joy and wonder in all God's works. They still find bugs fascinating, are able to marvel at the incredible sweetness of a ripe banana, and love to hear the tender beauty in a lullaby, even one sung by a tone-deaf parent. They are just beginning to experience the won-der and newness of God's creation. They already have the gift. It might be more appropriate to pray that they never lose it.

In Matthew's gospel Jesus tells his friends that, unless they "change and become like children," they will "never enter the kingdom of heaven" (18:3). There are so many signs of God all around us. There is so much to see. So much to hear.

Growing Old

If this can be—
I would go to you singing, Lord,
if that's allowed.
I owe you this for bliss
by Paraclete endowed,
the promised, preordained,
divine bequest I claimed,
hands clasped, head bowed.

—Unpublished poem by Dorsha Hayes,
friend and mentor of the author★

★ Dorsha Hayes was still working on this poem
shortly before her death at age ninety-four.

Reflections of a Septuagenarian

In January 1999 I turned seventy, one of those big birthdays. There's no way I can think of myself as middle-aged anymore. I'm not even sure whether I still fit in the gerontologists' kindly category of the "young old." Sixty or so years ago I was sure that, if I made it to the year 1999, life would be pretty much over. I would be a nice old lady, just waiting for the end—not much fun, not very interesting, and certainly not much of a challenge.

Today's reality is something else. Life is full, almost too full, lived in increasing awareness of my mortality. Even minimal competence in calculation tells me that my days are numbered. Of course, they have always been numbered, but we can live for decades denying this truth. But now I am sure, especially in that thin time just before dawn when God can seem so very close—or so very distant. I think of Sammy, the newest grandchild, and wonder whether I will be around to send him a high school graduation present. I wonder if I will see the wisteria, just beginning to wind itself around the oak in the front yard, reach the top and blossom lavishly. I wonder if I will have time to read all the books, see all the movies, write all the letters, preach all the sermons that seem so important to me now. Of course I won't. Maybe, with a little help, I'll make it to the graduation; and maybe the wisteria will grow at record speed. But in my heart I know that I am finite and my days are numbered.

The unanticipated fruit of this awareness is a new appreciation of the preciousness of each day. There is a fresh intensity in seeing, a consciousness of little things that would have gone unnoticed a few years ago. Much of this is sensory: there is delight in noticing tastes, sounds, sights, and smells that I have taken for granted for years. I decided this spring that a perfect strawberry is an undeniable proof of the existence of God. For backup proof, there's the glorious polyphonic music of Hildegard that pours from the CD player while I struggle to find the right word on the computer. There is such prodigality in God's creation, so much to savor and be grateful for. Along with my heightened appreciation of God's marvelous minutiae, I find in myself a new perspective about my own *stuff*. Tangible and intangible, there is still a lot to be let go.

I can't deny moments of apprehension. How will my earthly life end? How will I manage? Who am I to pontificate about living and aging? The time of trial, the one from which we pray to be spared, hasn't come yet. Yet I know that it will come, and I pray to be ready.

At seventy, I find that loving is easier. Grandparental love is careless. You might even say that its standards are low—we can love without wanting anything in return. We can love without worrying whether the recipient of our love ever learns the multiplication tables or holds down a job. (By the way, you don't have to be a grandparent to love this way.) I delight at being recognized as a pushover by babies and toddlers. It was a wonderful moment in the airport when I emerged from the jetway and a toddler lunged at me, yelling

"Nana!" His mother was embarrassed, but I thought it was great.

These days the picture is getting filled in, as the weaving of the tapestry is almost complete. I am filled with an amazing sense of connection. I am part of a large and all-embracing family—not just those related to me by blood or marriage, but all those related to me in baptism. I grow in awareness that in God's great economy nothing is wasted. Even painful loss bears fruit.

There is still a lot of work to be done. Now I can afford to give things away. I give away my time spent "in conversation"—I don't call it spiritual direction anymore. To be sure, I never accepted payment, but now it feels truly like a gift. My service in the parish that is now my home is also a gift to the church. Admittedly, being nonstipendiary permits a certain feistiness impossible in my younger days, but I rejoice at my acceptance into a vibrant team of clergy and lay ministers. Right now, I see no end to my active ordained ministry. I can always pray intercessions from my bed, if and when it comes to that.

I would like to be like my Great-Aunt Ellen, to become a spunky centenarian. But I know in my heart that today is all I have. And that is enough. God willing, if I were to address this topic as an octogenarian in 2009, I am sure that there will be a new vista with new challenges.

Notes from a Sojourner

Not long ago I moved from the spacious old, ghost-filled brownstone that I had occupied for nineteen years. The weeks before the actual move, when a team of muscular men swiftly emptied the rooms and crammed all my worldly goods into a shabby truck, were spent in sorting, weeding, packing, and reflecting. Perhaps not surprisingly, it was a profound spiritual exercise as well as a predictable physical challenge, as I dragged boxes of books from room to room and ran up and down the stairs countless times each day. (Brownstones are very vertical houses!) As I worked, I pondered the sermon that I was to preach on the Fourth Sunday after Pentecost. "Foxes have holes," Jesus tells his friends, "and the birds have their nests, but I have no place to lay my head." In other words, he is homeless, a sojourner at best, dependent on the hospitality of others—Mary and Martha, Zacchaeus, Simon the leper, and the little boy with five loaves and two small fish.

What irony to have his words running through my head as I contemplated my possessions! I had always thought of myself as relatively austere, certainly not acquisitive, so where had it all come from? Grandmother's good china, too elegant to be used since it isn't dishwasher-safe, must nevertheless be carefully packed for future generations. The linen closet bulged with more blankets and tablecloths than two people could possibly use, hearkening back to the days when my household was much larger. An impressive array of pots and pans recalled the time when I baked all the family's bread and regularly gave bountiful supper parties for the hungry college students in my classes. To say nothing of the mountain of books!

The work of sorting was like an archeological dig. Hour after hour and day after day, I took bits of my life in hand. There were a few baby clothes and toys, even some from my own childhood, and my children's favorite books, warped from two decades in the cellar. My wedding dress emerged from the long-unexplored back of the closet, ballet-length of soft blue lace, frugally chosen to look unwedding-like so that it could later double as an evening dress. (Was I ever really that tiny?) Boxes unopened from the last move revealed an accumulation of textbooks bearing my children's names. I found photographs and forgotten letters and felt the presence of my parents and grandparents as I sifted through them. A big box of lecture notes recalled my earlier life as a college professor—how long ago that was!—and a few cubic feet of notecards were the beginning of a book that never got written.

And all the while, Jesus' message was running through my mind: travel light, don't carry along a lot of things, just trust that there will be enough when you need it. Moths and rust had not corrupted all the stuff that filled my house, and no thief had been tempted to break in and steal. But I learned something about unused possessions: they become grimy, even when they are carefully put away. Despite their tangibility, they are impermanent. Mildew forms, and paper turns to dust. Old pictures—not antiques but just early

Polaroids—fade beyond recognition. As I filled large trash bags with the useless rubble that I had stockpiled, I realized, "Not to be used is to decay." It struck me that this was a powerful message of our transience and impermanence: what is true of mere objects must be even more true of us, our mental and spiritual gifts and energy. It's useless to store them up out of sight and mind—like my obsolete yogurt maker and a nonfunctioning clock—just in case we might use them some day.

Melancholy and exhilaration competed as I explored the layers of my past. I knew that I was saying goodbye to more than nineteen rich years in New York. I was saying goodbye to my children's childhood and to hoarded bits of my old identity. I was leaving a place I had loved, and I was trying to travel, if not so lightly equipped as Jesus prescribes to his disciples, at least not so encumbered as I might be. I began to enjoy finding things to get rid of. It became almost a game, accelerating as the moving day drew closer. The big black trash bags proliferated. I trundled load after load of usable clothing and bedding to the Salvation Army a few blocks away. The local branch library took a huge pile of books for its monthly fundraising sales. Toys, jigsaw puzzles, a pair of crutches, and other assorted oddments were simply set out by the sidewalk, there for the taking by the homeless and the affluent alike. The only object that didn't disappear overnight was the obsolete yogurt maker; I am convinced that the younger generation simply didn't know what it was.

Yet there was sadness beneath the exhilaration. Even though like the foxes and the birds I was far from homeless, I felt the chill bleakness of setting out for a new Promised Land. Nineteen years ago, the Upper

West Side of Manhattan had been Canaan, but gradually it had turned into Egypt. Now it was time to go,
and I wanted to hold on. Like the children of Israel
yearning for the leeks and cucumbers of Egypt, I was
pining in advance for authentic bagels and noisy sub-
ways. They complained to Moses: "If only we had meat
to eat! We remember the fish we used to eat in Egypt
for nothing, the cucumbers, the melons, the leeks, the
onions, and the garlic, but how our strength is dried up,
and there is nothing at all but this manna to look at"
(Numbers 11:4–6b). I was distinctly better off than the
children of Israel, but could "all this manna" possibly
suffice? Would I not soon yearn for more exotic fare?

It is hard to accept the fact that we are sojourners,
essentially homeless despite comfortable houses and
book-lined studies. Part of me wants to cling to the
noisy city that I had come to love and to resist the challenge of a new beginning. But the sojourner sees the
joy and the promise contained in that challenge: "Do
not remember the former things, or consider the things
of old. I am about to do a new thing; now it springs
forth, do you not perceive it?" (Isaiah 43:18–19a).

I can't imagine that my newly embraced Promised
Land will eventually turn into Egypt and that I will
have to set out once more. Surely not again! In the
meantime, I rejoice in the wonder of the New Thing
that even now springs forth.

The House I Live In

I still think of my present house as "new." Built in 1970, it hasn't been around long enough to accumulate the interesting flavors of other houses I have lived in—the hundred-year-old genteelly shabby brownstone on New York's Upper West Side, the austerely patrician seventeenth-century house in Zurich, the 1920s bungalow of my childhood, the ramshackle farmhouse in Jenkins Hollow. Unlike these others, this house isn't old enough to have ghosts. Thirty years in the life of a house is *nothing*.

So it surprised me the other day when I was forced to acknowledge that the quirkiness of the stairwell light switch can only be attributed to old age. Then I looked around and noticed that the laundry room floor looks pretty yucky and there's a crack in the front step.

I shouldn't have been surprised. After all, the Psalmist—whoever he, she, they were—reminds us of the transience of all things:

> In the beginning, O LORD, you laid the
> foundations of the earth,
> and the heavens are the work of your hands;
> They shall perish, but you will endure;
> they shall all wear out like a garment;
> as clothing you will change them,
> and they shall be changed. (Psalm 102:25–26)

Only God endures. Everything else gets old, loses its luster, and wears out. Even my "new" house.

Whenever I hear these verses, I am reminded of the urgent need to update my wardrobe: inevitably, what I think of as nearly new has become worn and shabby. Of course, there is nothing wrong with harboring a few old garments in the back of the closet. Comfortable and unpretentious, they may be fit for wear around the house on Saturdays. They might even be sufficiently presentable for a trip to the grocery store or post office. But eventually they must go—perhaps to serve as cleaning rags or more likely straight into the trash bin. I rarely salvage anything good enough for the parish clothing drive. The combination of innate Midwestern frugality plus growing up in the Depression makes reckless and premature disposal of outworn garments impossible. I hold on to them too long! I realized this long ago when the Salvation Army politely but firmly declined my gift of a winter coat that I had at last decided had to go!

I'm out of step in our society that values newness for its own sake. I don't want familiar products presented to me as new and improved. I am saddened by hollowed-out cities ringed with malls and even more saddened by the sight of the neglected, near abandoned malls that have lost their place in the pecking order. I manage to ignore the fashion industry that tries to convince me to discard last year's favorites in favor of the radically different. (If you wait long enough and don't gain any weight, everything comes around again.)

Most obviously, our society's obsession with newness is consumption-driven. The old must be discarded before it is worn out, to be replaced by the purportedly new and better. As an underachieving consumer, I can dissociate myself from such crassness. At a deeper level, though, I suspect that our insatiable appetite for the new is one way of coping with a fear of transience and death.

Old is one thing. Worn-out is quite another. What is truly worn-out is no longer useful. Nor viable.

A few years ago I was stranded in a Florida airport and picked up a book to while away the hours of waiting. It was Sherwin Nuland's *How We Die*. My choice was ironic since I was in the land of Juan Ponce de León, surrounded by other aging folk who were seeking youth or at least trying to hold on to life. I was actually one of the younger, more sprightly people in the waiting area. Had we been in Orlando, the airport population would have been leavened by the pilgrims to Disneyland.

Nuland is a tough writer, and his message is cool and clear: sooner of later, something is going to get us. One system or another will break down. Our bodies will wear out. Wryly, he observes:

> An octogenarian who dies of myocardial infarction is not simply a weather-beaten senior citizen with heart disease—he is the victim of an insidious progression that involves all of him, and that progression is called aging. The infarction is only one of its manifestations, which in his case has beaten out the rest, though any of the others may be ready to snap him up should some bright young doctor manage to rescue him in a cardiac intensive care unit.★

I found this to be strangely comforting. I will grow old and wear out like a garment. Like the stairwell light switch, my inner circuit breakers won't work so reliably

★ Sherwin Nuland, *How We Die* (New York: Vintage Books, 1995), 81.

or maybe they won't work at all. Like my laundry room floor, my looks will show wear and tear, to say nothing of neglect. Like some of those beloved garments in the back of the closet, my fabric will become thin and worn; eventually it won't be of much use to anyone, least of all to me.

I'm still pondering why I found Nuland's stark message comforting. His writing offered neither pretty pictures nor cheap comfort. The book should have been a real downer. But as I read it there in the bustling Tampa-St. Pete airport, I felt relief. I'll do my best to keep the garment serviceable and in good repair. I won't worry if it gets shabby and out of fashion. I hope and pray that I won't be troubled, either, when it's truly worn out and it's time to let it go.

Who Is That Person in the Mirror?

Every now and then, when I look in the mirror, I see the other Margaret Adah, my maternal grand-mother who died when I was fourteen. Faded old pictures show her as a beautiful young woman, but of course I knew her as a grandmother. A grandmother who wasn't into makeup and hairdressers. A grandmother whose face was etched with years of work and her share of hardship.

It startles me to see my grandmotherly self looking back at me. Inwardly I still feel thirty-something, forty-something at the most. I haven't accepted aging as my grandmother did. After she acquired the status of matron, she would never have worn bib overalls or waded in the river. It would never have occurred to her to sit on the floor to play with me. In fact, it wouldn't have occurred to her to play with me under any cir-cumstances. Her grandmotherly role was instruction: how to embroider and crochet, how to eviscerate a chicken (a skill I have never had to use), how to make piecrust. She seemed content to be old, even to enjoy it as it gave her justification for dropping out of the rat race and sitting in her rocker.

To be sure: grandmothers aren't what they used to be. Every now and then I take a look at *Modern Maturity,* the upbeat journal of the AARP. All the mod-ern and mature people depicted in those pages look awfully good—lithe and lean and frighteningly athletic. Even the models in the advertisements at the back of the magazine, those ads for electric scooters and incontinence aids, look awfully good. The magazines at the supermarket checkout are even worse. I'll never live up to those editors' idea of successful aging even if I join a gym this minute and engage a personal trainer. This is not my kind of aging, either. I'm somewhere between my grandmother who looked and acted every day of her age and those good-looking, handsomely dressed people playing golf and scuba diving as they enjoy their senectitude.

It still surprises me a bit to be seen as an old lady, to be told gently to "take my time" as I dig in my coin purse for exact change in the checkout line. The bus driver no longer asks to see my Medicare card when I drop two quarters through the slot. I was a trifle annoyed on a recent trip, however, when the flight attendant reseated me. I had been placed in the exit row, and without asking she was pretty sure that I would never get the emergency door open. I thought about inviting her to arm-wrestle. I also thought about asking the likelihood of our needing the emergency exit at all: most likely, we would either reach our destination without incident, or we would plummet from the skies into the North Carolina mountains. In either case, my services would not be needed. But instead, I docilely changed seats with a muscular youth.

Not so long ago I spent a few days in Cambridge, Massachusetts, a city where I spent five of the most important years of my life. There I earned a doctorate, met and married my husband—the one I still have— and bore my first child. I was petite and pretty, with short dark-blonde hair and a smooth, rosy complexion.

Maybe I looked something like my grandmother even then, like the vibrant woman who was young so long before I was born. As I made a nostalgic pilgrimage through Harvard Yard and around the Square, I watched the current crop of students. They were almost bursting with youth and intellectual intensity. I felt *very* old. They moved deferentially out of my path, and a few even smiled at me. I wanted to stop one of them—any one would have done—and tell them how I used to own this space, how these sidewalks and shops used to be mine, how I indeed thought that I owned the world, just as they claimed ownership now. I would tell them that somewhere on a remote closet shelf I still had a distinctive green Harvard bookbag, just like theirs. Like them, I had dragged it, full of books, from the massive library to my rented room. (I wouldn't think of using it now, even if I wanted to show off my academic roots—a shoulder bag is much easier on the back.) I wanted to tell them: "I wish you well. You may not believe it, but I know what it is like to be like you, to stand on tiptoe at the threshold of adulthood." I wanted to give them a grandmother's blessing. But instead I enjoyed my walk through the groves of academe, filled with benevolence and feeling as if I were somehow in disguise.

I love being my present age. There is great power and freedom in its powerlessness. I can avoid distasteful jobs by pleading decrepitude. I don't go to parties anymore unless I *really* want to. Most of the time, I can sleep with the alarm turned off. I can get into the movies for half-price. Anyone who eats at my table must be happy with my culinary peculiarities. Ditto anyone who sleeps in my guestroom—I am not Martha Stewart. On the street, I can smile uninhibit-

edly at babies and small children. No one would mistake me for a terrorist or a mugger.

And I really don't mind looking like the other
Margaret Adah. I could do a lot worse.

Diminishment

One of the rituals of middle-class well-baby care is the regular visit to the pediatrician, first monthly and then at increasing intervals. The high point, for the proud mother at least, after the baby has been inspected, poked, and prodded, is weighing and measuring. It is a sign of progress and indeed may be the only measurable sign of cooperation between mother and baby. The baby has done its part by eating, and the mother has conscientiously provided the fuel for growth.

I seem to recall that a thriving infant doubles its weight in the first six months and then accomplishes heaven-knows-what for the rest of that crucial year. Measuring length—height is hardly a meaningful concept in those early months—is more problematic than the relatively precise procedure of plunking a naked little body on a scale. Babies have a way of expanding and retracting, just when you want them to stretch out in a tidy, measurable way. I remember my shocked protest when the doctor announced that my wiggly second child had actually become an inch shorter since her previous visit. "Try again," I urged, "that simply can't be right." We all tried again, and—sure enough!—she had achieved a satisfactory growth rate.

Those days are long past. Now it's my turn to show up regularly at the doctor's office for routine maintenance. No longer is the aim to double my weight in the next six months or six years; it's good enough just to hold the line. Nor is there any expectation of adding inches to my height. Instead, we're just trying to hold on to what I already have.

Two years ago I encountered my first bone-density test. Now the flavor of the month in the monitoring of aging female bodies, it's a relatively new procedure. It's quick, painless, and doesn't even threaten your dignity: you stretch out—unlike the squirming baby—fully clothed while the technician fiddles with the controls on a machine straight out of *Star Wars*. The aim, of course, is not to measure growth but shrinkage. It's good news to hear that I've stayed the same, bad news to learn that I'm getting shorter.

So, a week or so after the test, I learned that I am no longer sixty-two inches high, tall, or long but rather a mere sixty-one and one-half. Which means, of course, that my sturdy peasant bones are not so sturdy as they used to be. They still feel big and strong to me, but they are melting away from within. My frame is diminished. No longer waxing, I am waning.

There are other signs, of course. My teeth, which look quite good to the casual observer, are a masterpiece of dental ingenuity. When I mention to my physician that my hair is falling out at a new and amazing rate, she gives me her patient look and reminds me that I am aging. When the liturgy calls for quick kneeling and graceful arising, I mutter a prayer—not to God, but to my increasingly recalcitrant knees: "Don't let me down. You can do it one more time." So far, they haven't let me down, but I know that the day is coming.

These are all *physical* signs of the diminishment that
age brings. They are significant, but up to now they
have not impeded me or caused me pain. At most, they
are signs, pointing me toward the ultimate diminishment that marks the end of earthly life.

In the final chapter of John's gospel, Jesus reminds
Peter of the inevitability of this diminishment:

> When you were young you fastened your belt
> about you and walked where you chose; but
> when you are old you will stretch out your arms,
> and a stranger will bind you fast, and carry you
> where you have no wish to go. (John 21:18,
> NEB)

I really don't mind losing some physical stature.
When you have hovered around five feet for seven-plus
decades, you are accustomed to living pretty close to
the ground. But there is that other dimension, intangible and imponderable, that defines me. At least, in my
limited and self-centered way, I *think* it defines me: I
want to hold on to the self that has nothing to do with
appearance or agility. I want to hold on to my life in all
its comfort, joy, and preciousness.

I cherish facility with words, my own joy in weaving them together and the even greater joy in reading
the words of others. I cherish all the gifts of the senses,
the tastes and smells and sights that enrich the most
ordinary day. A Mozart piano concerto is playing as I
write, thanks to the wonder of a computer that
includes a CD player among its built-in gadgetry. How
can I take it so for granted? How can I be so casual in
my choices—will this morning be a Mozart day, or will
I revel in Lotte Lenya's husky voice belting out coarse
lyrics from *Die Dreigroschenoper?* One of the spring's

first daffodils is in the tiny vase on my desk—such an amazing, startling yellow and such a wonderful shape! Perhaps most of all, I cherish memory, whether it is excavating the minutiae of family stories with my big brother or simply the ability to recall a few lines of poetry memorized sixty years ago.

I don't mind my newly spongy bones and thinning hair, but I want to hold on, hold on tight to life itself. I wonder what Peter thought when his loving and for-giving Teacher spoke such truth to him. Did he have a rejoinder? In the past he had been quick and decisive in his replies, swift to promise more than he could deliver. John doesn't tell us, but maybe this time he was willing to be silent. Maybe he could grasp that there was nothing to be said.

I'm not there yet, but I'm working on it.

Things I Will Never Do Again

Sometimes I catch myself thinking of things that I will never do again. Some of them are things that I have never done, so maybe they can be classified as "missed opportunities." There's a tinge of poignancy in some of these reflections, but mostly they bring a sense of relief.

I will never ride a bicycle again—except maybe a stationary one. Slow and always uneasy with traffic, I was never very good, but I managed to stay upright and even to enjoy leisurely rides on quiet streets and Cape Cod trails. That was several decades ago, and I have no desire to test my present balance and agility. By the same token, I will never rollerskate again. My last attempt, when I was a college sophomore, was a terrifying experience. So now I watch the young and limber whiz by on their rollerblades and offer a little prayer of thanks that I need not compete.

I fear too that I will never dance again. In my younger days I was tolerably adept at the fox trot and other archaic steps, thanks to an Arthur Murray course in my teens. My true forte, however, was the Viennese waltz, thanks not to the tutelage of Arthur Murray but my beloved German teacher. I was speedy, even reckless, as I let myself be whirled around the floor. Most recently, though, my only waltz partner has been my cat—now deceased. He seemed to enjoy moving with me through the house at a rapid one-two-three, one-two-three pace. The last time I danced on a real dance floor was at my son's wedding. I thought I was doing rather well, considering the alien music blasting from the speakers, until he muttered, "Ma, you're leading!" I'm sure that I was—maybe as a political statement about women's equality or maybe because, as his mother, I knew best. At a wedding last week, though, I didn't dance at all. Nobody asked me! Perhaps white hair and a clerical collar were a deterrent. So I sat on the sidelines with the bride's grandmother, a little disappointed and at the same time relieved since the music had gotten even more extraordinary since my son's wedding twelve years ago. And of course, I was no longer a sprightly sixty but a tough—and somewhat stiffer—seventy-something.

I'll never climb Old Rag. That's our landmark mountain here in Rappahannock County. Rough and craggy, it's the Everest that beckons the city folk to try their prowess at rock climbing. I've lived in Old Rag's shadow off and on for twenty-five years and have never been tempted to come closer. It's a relief now to know that I no longer need to make excuses, even to myself. I can just look at the majestic jagged profile across Mr. Buckner's meadow and murmur to myself, "Some poor fool's up there sliding around on the rocks. Hope he doesn't step on a rattler." Then I continue my walk on snake-free, level ground.

I doubt that I'll ever change another diaper. To be sure, Sarah was ninety. It's no wonder that Abraham fell on his face and laughed. And no wonder that Sarah laughed too. Barring miracles (for my generation) and accidents (for the younger generation), we have had our quota of babies, who are rapidly evolving into Big

People. While I'm happy to close the door on that part of my life, I wish now that I had kept count, although in my child-rearing days there was no time for such trifles. Changing diapers and—in the old, pre-Pampers days—washing them is valuable work for those who wish to cultivate humility. I'm delighted that I've done my share. I'm sure that I'm a better person for it.

I'll never worry about a prom date or indeed any other date again. When I was a junior in high school, all the boys were strong-armed by the principal into inviting a girl to the dance. So everyone had a date. I went with Robert, first cellist in the school orchestra. There was no romantic attraction between us, hardly even friendship. But we often made music together, as I accompanied him on his cello. Once we got to the prom we pretty much went our separate ways, but I was spared the shame of exclusion. The next year, that crucial senior year, was different: free market dating prevailed. I waited. And waited. No phone calls. No awkwardly, casually, or passionately delivered invitation in the hallways. Nothing. This may have been my first experience of failure. It was certainly an experience of powerlessness. I was sure that something was very wrong with me and that I was doomed to a life of rejection. I spent the evening of the prom on the living room sofa, alternately crying and reading *The Adventures of Sherlock Holmes*. Sherlock was always a consolation when I was a social failure. He would have loved me for my intellect—if he didn't ignore me completely.

So I offer another minor prayer of thanksgiving: I can forget about prom dates. Instead, I'll have an occasional lunch with my friends, male and female, and never again wait for the phone to ring with the invitation for The Great Date.

I'll never write another term paper. I have written so many highly disposable pieces, all the spiritless utterances ground out to satisfy academic requirements. When I went to seminary as a "mature student," I was appalled to realize that those precious years of learning would be punctuated by any number of little occasions of accountability. I had hoped to think about God on a cosmic scale, and instead I found myself writing a little of this and a little of that, never free to follow the call to plunge into the depths. My words seemed shallow and evasive. They seemed like busy work. But I was a good girl so I played the game. After all, I wanted to graduate.

I remember well the last term paper of my academic career. It was for a delightful course on English Christian literature of the seventeenth century, the era of Donne, Herbert, Milton, and Bunyan. A small group of us sat around a seminar table and read and talked. For the first time, I even enjoyed *Paradise Lost*. The only piece of tangible work required was a twenty-page paper on a subject of my choice. It should have been sheer joy after three years of carefully coloring within the academic lines. But I couldn't face it! I calculated my grade point average, a degrading act for a fifty-four-year-old former academic, and realized that I could graduate even if I failed the course. I was tempted, but I remained a good girl to the end. I even enjoyed writing the paper. Sort of. But never again!

I can't be too rueful about the things that I will never do again. There is too much still to do.

Making It All Come Out Even

I learned to cook, really cook, when I was fifteen. Before that, I had survived an obligatory eighth-grade home economics class, where the shortages of World War II along with the general poverty of the Kansas City school system severely limited our raw materials. While we studied maps of animals showing where the various cuts of meat come from, there was, of course, no meat in our classroom. So I added this information to my stash of theoretical knowledge, which maybe someday would be useful. I learned to make a variety of dishes that I have never been tempted to repeat. Everything seemed to be white, bland, and lumpy—tapioca pudding, junket (does that still exist?), and thick white sauce, rather like library paste and used to disguise the color and taste of vegetables. Things were better at home, where I was welcome in the kitchen and—in those carefree days of calorie uncon-sciousness—developed what the old-timers called "a light hand with pastry."

Reality set in when I was fifteen: my mother was hospitalized for three weeks and then began a long period of convalescence at home. I became the family meal planner, shopper, and cook. I can't remember where the groceries came from, but I must have got them at the corner store on the way home from school. Wartime rationing was no problem; I managed the little coupon books comfortably and wondered what everyone was complaining about. The preparation of individual dishes was likewise no problem. Anyone who could read could follow a recipe, so culinary procedures were no more difficult than an experiment in the science lab.

The challenge lay in having everything ready at once, the hot dishes hot and the cold dishes cold. Over the decades this has become second nature to me, but I will never forget my struggles to make it all come out even—the string beans still green and crisp rather than limp and gray, the roast neither raw nor incinerated. My mind and my reflexes were forced into unfamiliar paths as I scrambled to think of several things—trivial things!—at once. It felt as if preparing a meal demanded the skills of a juggler, mentally and all too often physically as well.

In this my eighth decade I find myself remembering the fifteen-year-old cook-juggler. Now it seems important to make my life come out even. I want to cross the threshold with my desk tidied up so that even the unbelievably messy middle drawer is a model of neatness. I want all the letters written, even those I have been neglecting for years. I want to leave my refrigerator clean, with no mysterious sticky places in remote corners and no moribund cucumbers in the vegetable bin. And likewise the oven—I would leave it crud-free and sparkling.

More importantly, I want to have said everything that needs to be said. I want to ask forgiveness of those I have wronged or diminished or taken for granted. I want to forgive those people who have wronged me, not forgive them in a pinched, grudging way but with the extravagantly generous abandon of someone who finally sees the Big Picture. I want to ask my children to pardon my impatience and clumsiness in mothering them. I want to tell my husband that maybe his way of loading the dishwasher was almost as good as mine. I want to tell my grandchildren all the family stories that I have been saving until they had time to listen. They aren't going to have time, and mine is running out.

I want to be sure that I have said "I love you" to all the people whose love I take for granted.

So I have this vision of my life coming to a tidy end, all *t*'s crossed and all *i*'s dotted. Bach managed to bring a great harmonious chord out of the complexity of his fugues. Why can't I do that with my life? After all, I learned long ago how to make it all come out even in the kitchen.

Even as I cling to the fantasy, I know that it won't work. The Christian story is full of surprises, twists, and reversals, beginning with the surprise of the resurrection. The civil and religious authorities must have felt that they had settled the matter once and for all, definitively if cruelly, at Golgotha. The disciples must have thought that they had lived through a nightmare interlude and now order was being restored, when the risen Christ invited them to breakfast on the shore of the Sea of Tiberias. Even when their Teacher left them again, there must have been some sense of finality, that now the surprises had stopped and that they more or less understood their next steps. Now they could make it all come out even.

But the surprises didn't stop. Haven't stopped. The Holy Spirit is not only the most mysterious, least understood member of the Trinity; she is also the most untidy and least predictable. And despite all outward semblance of order, our human lives are equally untidy and unpredictable. What a rich mix! The anxious me may yearn to make it all come out even, to present my life as a neatly wrapped package, but I know that I am still a work in progress. I might as well give up the dream of orchestrating all my messy bits and pieces into a perfect whole. It's not going to happen on this side of the threshold.

Work

God give me work
Till my life shall end
And life
Till my work is done.*

—*On the grave of Winifred Holtby,
novelist, 1898–1935*

---

* *The Oxford Book of Prayer*, ed. George Appleton (New York: Oxford University Press, 1986), 117.

Retirement

Now that I have been officially retired for five years, I am ready to make some pronouncements. The memory of my years of gainful employment, by which I mean a title on my door and an officially sanctioned place in the institutional pecking order, is still fresh enough. At the same time, the novelty of seemingly unstructured time hasn't worn off: I continue to marvel that on some days I rise at five o'clock to catch a plane and on others I luxuriate under the blanket until eight. As the descendent of Midwestern farm folk, I can't imagine sleeping much later, barring coma or some similarly disabling condition.

So now I am ready to reflect on what it means to be "retired." I found some interesting bits in my trusty Webster's, meanings well beyond the mere cessation of turning up at the office, parish, or school every day. To retire can mean "to withdraw from action or danger, to march away from the enemy." Prudence, if I recall correctly from Systematic Theology I, is the foundation of the theological virtues. Retiring in this sense certainly calls for prudence—knowing when enough is enough, knowing when continued effort is counterproductive, simply knowing when it is time to quit. As a teacher, I think I knew this when I contemplated my dog-eared lecture notes and old syllabi. The students weren't complaining, at least not in my presence, but teaching my courses brought me no surprises and precious few new insights. I recognized the symptom. After all, I had "retired" once before, twenty years earlier, when I left my secular teaching career to enter seminary. It was time to stop coasting along paths worn smooth by much travel and move in a new direction. Maybe it was even time to stop relying on old knowledge, bits of intellectual baggage safely preserved in the tired piles of papers cluttering my office. Maybe it was time to abandon the safety of lecture notes and embark on the search for wisdom.

But "to withdraw from action or danger, to march away from the enemy"—could that be what my retirement was about? I am awed by the courage of teachers and clerics who have persisted in their pursuit of truth and the proclamation of the gospel despite the very real possibility of martyrdom. But teaching in an Episcopal seminary never felt particularly dangerous, and despite faculty politics and rivalries, the "enemies" among my colleagues did not pose such a menace that I would be tempted to march away. Nevertheless, the dangers were real. Perhaps the greatest, most menacing enemy was *acedia,* the tedious, indeed boring sin of sloth. Woody Allen has said that ninety percent of life consists of just showing up. Well, over the years I had become expert at just showing up. Maybe I could convince myself that this was good enough, that it could pass for passionate devotion to my calling, so long as one did not look too closely.

After all, my days were full. There were meetings to attend, lots of meetings! Over the years, I have come to realize that there is, in fact, only one meeting—the official gatherings of the local PTA, the counsels of vestries and dioceses, the faculty meetings of almost any august institution of higher learning, the conclaves of businesses large and small, maybe even the cabinet meetings in the Oval Office all bear a remarkable resemblance to one another. One of the joyful acts of purgation when I left the office that I had occupied for fourteen years was to shred the minutes of several hundred faculty meetings. They were virtually interchangeable and utterly lacking in salacious, spicy tidbits, so in many ways shredding them was an act of supererogation.

Yet another meaning offered by my dictionary is "to withdraw from circulation or from the market." Maybe that's what I'm doing. I have no desire to become invisible or inactive; but even as I continue to circulate, I rejoice that there are many games I no longer have to play. When I find myself over-committed, it's my own fault. I no longer clean up after other people, so expect no pity if I find myself painted into a corner. I am no longer even remotely tempted to compete for titles or status. I'll never be a cardinal rector or, for that matter, even a sparrow rector. I cheekily call bishops by their Christian names. Comfortably removed from the fracas, my jersey having been retired, I can sit on the sidelines and enjoy the game.

Being retired means that I no longer have a job. Being retired means that I can get on with my work.

My Little Room

O ne of my least favorite gospel messages is the ongoing commandment—implicit if not explicit—to keep on the move. Jesus the itinerant expected, indeed, insisted that his friends share his homelessness. "Follow me!" he invited and commanded, even if this meant leaving nets and ploughs and households behind.

This is a hard teaching for someone who is an inveterate nester, for someone like me who clings to the illusion of permanence and who resists embracing the reality of transience that is the life of a sojourner.

Like the phoebes who nest under the eaves in Jenkins Hollow, I am strongly identified with my nest, which may seem unimpressive to the neutral observer. I like to think that I am more realistic or perhaps a better planner than the phoebes. For years they created a rickety structure attached to the front porch light. None of us—neither the humans nor the frenetic birds—found that arrangement satisfactory. When we screened in the porch, they moved to a spot right over the screen door. They were clearly devoted to their new housing and visibly annoyed that we insisted on using the door. Now they have moved for a third time to a spot under the eaves. I think that we can now coexist comfortably.

I have no idea of the spiritual or emotional drain on these extraverted little birds, as they left their old nest and scrabbled around to create a new one, but I know that it was hard work.

Three years ago I returned to St. Columba's, where my official title is Associate Rector but my real role is Resident Crone. I didn't need much office space since I (and my desktop) live just a five-minute walk away. All I wanted was a little room where I could visit with people.

The rector was apologetic when he showed me the only available space—an eight by twelve, windowless room with cinder block walls and harsh fluorescent light. It was currently a storeroom, but at least it had a ventilating system since it had originally been intended for an office.

I fell in love with it at first sight.

There followed the delightful work of nest building. Karen, the property manager, found some tolerably decent furniture—three chairs, a bookcase, and a cupboard. A few lamps. A colorful cotton rug. The space began to feel like home when I added the favorite icons that had been part of my office at the seminary—the Rublev Trinity, the Virgin of Vladimir, and of course my fellow grandmother, St. Anne. I put the little Tyrolean peasant crucifix in its usual place on the wall beside my chair, where I could casually put my hand on it when needed. The dark little room couldn't support a living plant, but dried flowers and greenery brought a touch of the outdoors. (Eucalyptus lasts forever!)

The storeroom had become an inviting quiet place, sometimes referred to by my colleagues as "Lady Margaret's cell." I could almost feel its transformation as more and more prayers soaked into the cinderblocks. Like the foxes and the birds, I had my place of sanctuary.

But nothing is permanent. The space in the parish hall is being reconfigured, and my little room is destined to disappear. In the next few days its walls will be knocked out, and it will be absorbed into the big meeting room next door. As a consolation prize, I have been promised a room with a window, a new carpet, and maybe some really comfortable chairs.

Yesterday I cleared out my cell so that the demolition can begin. It didn't take long at all: in thirty minutes it was a bleak, ugly little space again. The icons were carefully tucked in my shopping cart, to be stored at home until my new room is ready in a month or so. In the interim, I will perch in whatever space is available to do my visiting.

As I walked home dragging my shopping cart full of holy pictures, I found myself remembering old nests long dismantled. As a very small child, I could spend hours playing under my grandfather's desk. My dolls and I fit in there quite cozily. That desk is in a corner of my study now. I crawl under it occasionally when the increasingly rare urge to dust comes upon me, but it isn't a comfortable fit anymore. I remembered my beloved room in a seventeenth-century house in Switzerland, full of dark massive furniture, with a tile stove for heating in the corner. It looked out on a square with an old fountain that splashed and whispered day and night. I remembered the bedroom of my girlhood, a thoroughly ordinary room but filled with the smell of honeysuckle on hot summer nights. I remembered grim, overheated college dorm rooms and near-slum graduate student apartments. Over the decades I have built a lot of nests, less frantically than the phoebes under the eaves. Some of them I have abandoned with joy and relief, some with tears.

I look forward to building my nest again in a few weeks. Maybe I can even adapt to the decadent idea of a cell with a window.

My Day Job

No one ever told me about one of the benefits of being retired and theoretically over the hill: now I can settle down and get on with my real work. No one expects me to turn up regularly at the workplace at nine o'clock, nor am I responsible for budgets and office supplies. I haven't prepared a syllabus in years. In my parish, where my work often takes me out of the city, I am a clerical Scarlet Pimpernel—now you see her, now you don't. At home my standards of housekeeping have relaxed to a level that would horrify my grandmother. There is no one whom I particularly want to impress, so I am free to cultivate my introversion and other eccentricities. Theoretically, I am retired, which I once thought meant long days of lolling on the sofa, watching the soaps, and eating bonbons.

I was wrong. Instead I am freed up to do the work I love. I spend a lot of time engaged in the ministry of spiritual direction—though I wish that it were called something else, as my discomfort is growing with the rather clinical terminology that has come to surround this holy work. I prefer to think of it as a ministry of presence or—less elegantly—as a ministry of hanging out with my fellow pilgrims. The people who seek me out are my friends, not my clients. I am not even sure how many of them there are, for my work could in no way be called a "practice." Many of them are parish-

ioners, but others come from "outside," from the
Washington community or from considerable distances. Some come so regularly that I can almost set my
watch by their appearance, but others check in now
and then. There are some whom I see only once.

And what do we do? We sit together in my little
room in the parish and visit.

This unassuming little word, rooted in and related to
the Latin *videre,* really describes our time together: we
pray, we talk, we listen, we share comfortable silence,
and most importantly, we strive to see clearly. The great
underlying question in all our words and silences is this:
Where is God in this person's life? Where is the Holy
Spirit active in the here-and-now, in the joys and sor-
rows and hassles of ordinary living? What is the vision,
perhaps barely hidden and waiting to be claimed?

My job is to listen and to ask the occasional question. I am not there to solve problems or make another
person over in my image. The best and indeed only gift
that I can offer is my full attention and my distanced
love. I am unable to do this kind of listening with family and close friends because we have too much baggage and too many claims on each other. Our love is
anything but distanced: it is delightfully or annoyingly
entangled in all sorts of stuff. With my visitors, however, my love is distanced because I want nothing from
them except their prayers. Most decidedly I do not
want monetary remuneration. The idea of accepting
payment for being prayerfully present to another is
repellent to me. More to the point, my anxiety level
would soar if I were constantly asking myself, "Is this
person getting his money's worth? Am I really worth
$25 or $50 or $100 an hour?" Even more to the point,
I would be in grave danger of forgetting an essential

truth: that I am not the star or even a major player, but rather both of us are waiting upon the action of the Holy Spirit.

Every now and then I remember that I used to direct a training program in spiritual direction and I don't know whether to smile or sigh at what my students would think if they were evaluating my work. It's not a performance and certainly no feat of professional bravura. It's just sitting there in my quite comfortable chair, with no expectations and no agenda, and doing my best to honor the person in the other chair. I can't decide whether it is terribly hard or terribly easy work, but I know that it sustains me.

It continues to amaze me that anyone would trust me so much. Soul-work is so tender! The secrets of the heart, our God-secrets, are our deepest and most precious. The good news is that this work is not limited by the age of the practitioner. The holy listeners of the Egyptian desert were commonly addressed as Abba or Amma, Old Man or Old Woman. I'm not so sure about Old Woman—I confess to a bit of lingering vanity— but I would be delighted to be addressed as Amma. The vision needed for our visiting has nothing to do with performance on the ophthalmologist's eye chart. Physical agility is not required. So I can picture myself never retiring from this wondrous work of accompanying others as they find and are found by God. They may have to speak a little louder, and I may nod off from time to time. They will have to be patient with my repetitiousness and forgive me if I need to be reminded of details.

But I think that the quality of my work will improve with age. For an Amma, I'm still on the young side.

My Other Day Job

At heart I am a nester. Home decoration is not one of my gifts or passions, so the style of my beloved nests might best be designated as hodge-podge. I cling to the safety of familiar places, not because they are especially grand or beautiful, but because they are home. Leaving them for a new place, even when I am eager to move on, is always a foretaste of dying, a painful ripping up of my roots. I've never been in prison, but I can well imagine that I would look with anguish at the warden when she entered my cell to announce my release. I'm sure that I would have turned it into a meager nest of some sort and would abandon it with regret even as I longed for freedom.

So my present work comes as a surprise. I have become a circuit rider. When I am not at home, nestled in my study at my faithful desktop or sitting in conversation with someone in my little room at the church down the street, I am on the road. Throughout all my years of schooling, from my four-room elementary school right down to seminary attended in my fifties, the same comment recurred on my report cards: "You should speak up more in class." I'm not sure how it happened, but now I talk all the time. So retirement finds me on the road, offering workshops, conferences, and retreats. I'm waiting for a report card that says,

"That's fine. You can quit. You have probably spoken up enough."

I discovered Sherlock Holmes when I was about thirteen. After that I entertained myself during obligatory study hall by reading the *Complete Works,* all one thousand-plus pages of them, over and over. At one point I could quote accurately and identify quotations from the most obscure of the stories. That gift—or obsession—has receded from my memory, but one scene, a conflation from a number of stories, remains fixed.

In the Baker Street flat the faithful and silent Mrs. Hudson would have served breakfast and cleared away the dishes. Holmes would be lounging around, scraping away at his violin, bored and languid. Then he would be called to a case and spring to life. "Quick, Watson! The game's afoot."

My present life in retirement is pleasant. There are no deadlines, as there were in the days of syllabi and budgets. There are no great demands on me from an institution that wants its money's worth. I am free to putter around the house, to mosey down the street to the mailbox, and—when I am feeling energetic—to walk to the busy avenue. There I can sample the gourmet cheese in the upscale grocery, get some toothpaste and flashlight batteries at the drugstore, visit my old friend the dry cleaner who remembers me from forty years ago, and rent a movie from my new friend Damian. It's a good life.

Laziness sets in. I ask myself: why am I still pushing myself? Why do I continue to put myself on the line? Why not stay home, read novels, and use the computer for playing solitaire?

But whenever I snap the suitcase shut and head for the airport, I almost always experience a Sherlock Holmes moment. The game's afoot! I'm not off on a junket to solve crime but rather to experience the church in all its richness and wonder. I find that I sleep well wherever I am billeted—in monasteries and convents, diocesan conference centers, motels, the occasional rather precious bed and breakfast, and even more rarely in an elegant hotel. I have to remind myself not to make my bed when I am lodged in a commercial establishment—monastic habits die hard. I eat catfish in Louisiana, fried okra in North Carolina, vegemite in England and equally unpalatable marmite in Australia. I have sampled emu in South Africa. (It tastes like beef.) Mostly I work among Anglicans, but my travels take me also to Baptists, Presbyterians, Methodists, Lutherans, and Roman Catholics.

The wonder of my life as a circuit rider is this: I am convinced that I have a glimmering of what the early church must have been like. I arrive in a strange city, knowing no one. At most, I have exchanged letters or e-mails, perhaps an occasional telephone call with my hosts. I am met at the airport. Astonishingly, there is instant recognition: we always find each other without benefit of signs or paging over the airport loudspeaker.

And then I am home, even thousands of miles from my own familiar nest. The circle expands to take me in, and I feel safe and loved among people whom I have never seen before and whom I will probably never see again. For a little while, I am one of them.

I have been richly privileged. I have felt at home in a South African monastery and on the plains of Nebraska, in a Roman Catholic convent in Alabama and among the Episcopal Church Women of Northern

Michigan. Home turns out to be wherever two or three are gathered in the name of Christ. Home is to be found in all sorts of unlikely places.

Someday, maybe sooner and maybe later, this will all be too much for my aging body. Then I'll have time to catch up on my reading. And there are a lot of movies I still haven't seen.

Priorities for Shepherds

In Luke's gospel Jesus tells the story of the sheep who got lost. Not a bad sheep, I'm sure, but stupid and careless. The Good Shepherd leaves his ninety-nine responsible nibblers and goes in search of the lost one. I picture the shepherd clambering over rocks and climbing steep hills, risking at least exhaustion or a sprained ankle. When he finds the lost sheep, he is overjoyed and carries it home on his shoulders.

This is a story of caring, tenderness, and generosity. The shepherd goes to extra trouble and clearly didn't count the cost: he took a real risk in leaving the ninety-nine to look for the errant one.

Mine is the confession of a Bad Shepherd. My experience turns the story upside-down.

Just as in the real estate business location is everything, so in ministry—lay and ordained—motivation is everything. Ideally, we are able to forget ourselves and all possible rewards and satisfaction. We do our best and do not expect applause. After all, we have no evidence that the faithful shepherd was welcome when he returned with the straggler. Maybe his friends wondered why he had bothered to search for it instead of cutting his losses. Maybe no one even noticed that he had been gone.

Recently I gave a workshop. It was sold out. People were more than ready to like me, to like what I said, and to go home feeling that it had been a good experience. For three days we danced together, spiritually if not literally. The participants assiduously took notes while I talked, cooperated graciously in small group exercises, and ended by giving me a standing ovation.

I was walking on air. I was also working hard at not taking the adulation too seriously, working hard at my "aw shucks, gee whiz" response, trying to be a sort of spiritual Jimmy Stewart, who charmed a nation for decades with his homespun humility. But deep down inside, I was lapping it up. I was loving the warm experience of being loved. Even then, I knew that I was more than slightly in danger of forgetting my own small place in God's great economy.

Then the program ended with the exchange of hugs and e-mail addresses. I modestly thanked all the people who were so effusively thanking me. The crowd thinned, then disappeared, and I sat in the lobby of the conference center and waited for my transportation to the airport. While I waited, I leafed through a great pile of mauve papers, the evaluations filled out by the program participants. If anything, my glow of satisfaction increased as I repeatedly read "excellent" in the space for rating the presenter. I glowed even more as I read the comments, extolling my warmth, my accessibility, my wit, and my holiness. I was hot stuff! God was lucky to have me on God's lecture circuit!

Then near the bottom of the heap, my stock plummeted. For this program participant, I was rated "fair-to-poor" as a presenter. Maybe I was a fairly good writer, the disgruntled participant wrote, but it just didn't carry over in person. Clearly I was an introvert, inhibited in the extreme. All in all, the days at the workshop had been a disappointing experience.

I remembered her: we had chatted during one of the breaks. She was an articulate woman, focused rather narrowly on her own approach to our topic, with a bit of an edge to her, but seemingly open and friendly. I hadn't felt great affinity between us, but I hadn't felt hostility, either. Now her intensity took me aback. She hadn't liked me! Worse, she had sat there for hours on end disliking me, maybe hating me!

I was surprised, hurt, outraged. How dare she! How could she fail to recognize a stellar performance, especially when everyone else had leaped to their feet to applaud?

The longer I reflected on this one negative response, tucked in a great sheaf of adulation, the more I was surprised—not at the disappointed program participant, but at myself. Why and how could a few sharp words outweigh ninety-plus love letters from my fans? Why did I remember that one brief page? Why did it overshadow everything that had gone before—the candid give-and-take of discussion periods, the easy laughter at just the right places in my lectures, the earnest conversations over meals, the spontaneous friendliness that had characterized the workshop?

I like to think of myself as a humble follower of the Good Shepherd, happy to put self aside as I scramble through rough terrain and smooth in emulation of him. I like to think that I have my priorities straight—that my work is not about me or about my own satisfaction, but about the Good News of God's prodigal love. So it pains me and shames me to be caught out in pursuit of selfish goals, to find *myself* lost and in need of rescue.

I doubt that I will meet this woman again. In a way, I wish that I would, even though I am sure that she would scare me and make me self-conscious. I would like to thank her—not for her tips on public speaking or guidance on how better to present myself in large groups, but for the powerful reminder that I am a Bad Shepherd. Or, more charitably, that I am at best an Apprentice Shepherd, Junior Grade.

It's all too easy to forget who my boss is. My real boss isn't my bishop or even the church herself. My real boss is certainly not the people who engage me to entertain or enlighten them. My real boss is the Shepherd who is willing to clamber over the rocks and up the cliffs, then to disentangle the lost sheep from the thicket and carry it home. Rejoicing. Without a thought of thanks from the rescued one or the ninety-nine left to fend for themselves. That Good Shepherd probably doesn't have time to read the evaluations.

Hospital Corners

It is a tradition of monastic hospitality that, before a guest departs, she makes up the bed with fresh linens and offers a prayer for the next occupant of the room. Not long ago I found a slightly grouchy entry in one of my old journals: "June 9, 6:45 A.M. Bed is remade for the next retreatant. Hope s/he appreciates the hospital corners." I always land in a bed made by someone who has no clue. Bedmaking is a humble, invisible art, soon to be a lost art. Even as I profess to be above such petty concerns, I confess to considerable fussiness about sleeping conditions. Just as I scorn hard, gray tomatoes and iceberg lettuce in my sandwich, I am distressed by floppy sheets.

In these days of contour sheets, designed to provide a taut, smooth surface with minimal effort and skill on the part of the bedmaker, hardly anyone remembers how to do hospital corners. Indeed, I rarely call on this particular skill except when I hang out among frugal monastics who are still using linens acquired in the days of Father Founder, way back before World War II.

That's when I learned to be fussy about bedmaking. The war—for my generation, The War—began when I was in the eighth grade. Kansas City was far from the front lines, but Midwesterners are cautious folk. Roscoe Brown, the biology teacher who lived across the street, was appointed air raid warden for our block.

He took the responsibility seriously, at least for a while, but then lapsed back into his role of mere neighbor as he stopped making official visits. The Camp Fire Girls embarked on a knitting project, turning out drab brown squares of an afghan for the wounded. The war ended or maybe I abandoned the Camp Fire Girls before I turned in a satisfactory square, but I plugged away doggedly, knitting and purling, dropping stitches, and beginning anew.

The war came to the classroom. I'm not sure how the curriculum was affected for the boys. Maybe it was enough that sooner or later they would receive that ominous letter from the draft board, beginning with the deceptively friendly "Greetings." We girls, however, were being prepared to maintain the homefront through any dangers, toils, or snares that might befall us. A first aid course replaced one six-week unit of physical education. That was an interesting, even exotic experience. We bandaged each other heavily; to this day, pictures of mummies recall those exercises for me. On the gym floor we practiced artificial respiration— this was before CPR and the Heimlich maneuver. We readied ourselves to treat all sorts of catastrophic injury: we learned nothing so banal as removal of splinters, but I used to know how to deal with unfortunates who had been struck by lightning. To our disappointment, we were never permitted to take a door from its hinges so that we could practice transporting those with suspected spinal fractures—that would have been a challenging and memorable session.

The unit on home nursing was much less exciting since we skipped the section on delivering babies at home, but it was undoubtedly more useful. We learned a lot about basic hygiene; I'm sure this is where I became a compulsive hand-washer. We learned how to read a thermometer, a skill for which I am still grateful even though it is scarcely needed in these digital days. The high point of the class was the day we learned how to bathe a bedfast patient without flooding the sick-room. As probably the most docile and compliant in a roomful of docile and compliant girls, I was selected to be the "patient" for that demonstration by our Red Cross instructor. The experience didn't quite scar me for life, but it was mortifying at the time.

And we learned to make beds! Properly! Neatly! With geometric precision, the tucked-in sheets pre-cisely angled at forty-five degrees! This was the impor-tant learning that has remained part of me. More than any other task of preparation, I love to make the beds when I am getting ready for houseguests, especially for visiting children and grandchildren, anticipating their sense of comfort and safety. It doesn't matter that they have no idea of the thoughts (and occasional prayers) that get woven into the work of my hands.

It seems a great leap from my guestroom to the Rule of St. Benedict, that tiny book, compiled cen-turies ago for monks, men whose lives were different from mine in almost every imaginable way. Yet one of Benedict's claims to distinction is his elevation of hum-ble work to a high place in the human value system. His inclusion of manual labor as part of the Rule was a way of sanctifying the ordinary, of reminding us of the potential holiness of the material, of reminding us that the work of our hands can be sanctified when it is approached in the Spirit of God.

The cellarer, who bore the responsibility of keeping ordinary life running smoothly on a parallel track to the community's primary work of prayer, had "charge of everything." He was responsible for all the *impedimenta* of daily living—not vestments, paintings, and jeweled chalices, but pots and pans, hoes and hammers. And he was to treat all entrusted to him with reverence. Benedict writes: "Let him regard all the utensils of the monastery and its whole property as if they were the sacred vessels of the altar. Let him not think that he may neglect anything."*

Thomas Merton wrote somewhere that the essence of the Benedictine ethos is "doing ordinary things quietly and perfectly for the glory of God." This gives me pause. Maybe my vision is too limited. Perhaps I should lift my eyes from the mattress and approach my other simple tasks in the Benedictine spirit. Emptying the dishwasher, one of the most boring bits of my housewifery, can be sanctified if I remember to give thanks for the dishes, the food that was on them, the loved ones who ate from them, the hot water that cleaned them. Scrubbing the bathroom sink and the kitchen floor? Sorting and folding the laundry? Yes, these jobs can be done quietly and perfectly for the glory of God.

But I draw the line at washing windows and sewing on buttons. As of now, I can't imagine how such tedious jobs can be sanctified. But maybe I'll grow in holiness.

---

* *St. Benedict's Rule for Monasteries,* trans. Leonard J. Doyle (Collegeville, MN: The Liturgical Press, 1948), 49.

Touch and See

Jesus said to Thomas,
"Put your finger here and see my hands.
Reach out your hand and put it in my side."
(John 20:27a)

The disciples had hidden, locked themselves in a room because they were afraid. I wonder how long they had been there and whether or when they planned to get on with their lives. The locked room must have become a kind of tomb as they huddled together, paralyzed in their inactivity and hopelessness. I always picture it as hot and cramped, a place that is no-place, with mortal fear lurking just outside the door. My own experience of hiding is limited to the pleasurable thrills of childhood games of hide-and-seek; only in imagination can I glimpse what it must be like to listen breathlessly for footsteps and to wonder if my fragile cover will be ripped away in the next moment.

Suddenly Jesus is there. John doesn't tell us how he entered: he is simply there. The disciples, ever slow on the uptake, don't recognize him until he identifies himself by showing them his wounded hands and side.

Thomas was not present in that closed-up room. Where was he? Because he did not hide in fear, should we perhaps call him Courageous Thomas rather than the unkind epithet of Doubting Thomas? When his friends told him, "We have seen the Lord," he refused to believe his eyes alone and demanded to touch and probe Christ's wounded body.

Jesus' response to his doubt is an invitation. "Put your finger here and see my hands. Reach out your hand and put it in my side." This is a powerful invitation to come close and to experience his physical presence, his physical realness. He is saying, "Look closely. Be at home with me. Don't be afraid to touch me— you will neither hurt nor offend me."

The disciples, and especially Thomas, are urged to look at his wounds to make sure that they are in the presence of Christ—not a ghost, not an imposter, but their Friend and the Teacher himself. Had the disciples been brought up like most of us, taught that it's not polite to stare, particularly not to look closely at the hurts, wounds, and distortions that afflict our brothers and sisters? And were they, like us, schooled to be cautious about touch? Jesus urges them to probe his wounds. This is not a tentative little poke, but the kind of almost rough, exploratory touching we experience from babies and small children.

Nearly fifty years ago in another life, I worked as Girl Friday for a wise psychiatrist whose patients were sick and deeply troubled children. I shall never forget his dictum: "Good mothers tend to be a little bit messy. At least, their grooming isn't perfect." He knew that the touch of the small child, seeking assurance of safety and love, should not be hampered by warnings not to spoil Mummy's makeup or displace her carefully arranged hair. Jesus, our Teacher and good Friend, would pass my boss's test for a loving, embracing presence. He wanted the disciples to go beyond appearances and to know him.

Most of us present carefully prepared façades. At least, I do. The self we offer to others is not the product of conscious deception, but we have to be careful that no one disturbs the meticulously maintained surface. The message is implicit: "Don't look too closely at my wounds, please. And by all means feel free to touch me, but don't do the spiritual equivalent of spoiling my makeup or mussing my hair—of cracking my surface."

But Jesus is saying, "Be at home with me, and don't be afraid to touch me. You will neither hurt nor offend me."

He is setting us an example, but at the same time inviting us into ever-greater intimacy with him. He greets our fear and disbelief with loving acceptance, assuring us that he doesn't mind our questions and our probing, This gospel is no ghost story, some kind of holy *Twilight Zone* episode divorced from physical reality. Rather, it is an invitation to come close, close enough to see the wounds and feel his risen presence.

Jesus' appearance in the midst of his frightened friends is a story of Incarnation, a reminder of the wonderful fact that God came and comes among us, experiencing and loving our humanity. We are easily aware of this at Christmas, when we hear that "the Word became flesh and dwelt among us, full of grace and truth." Then the churches fill, and even nonbelievers are drawn instinctively by the powerful image of God coming among us in the perfection, loveliness, and vulnerability of a baby. Good Friday is about the Incarnation too: Jesus on the cross is an icon of suffering, a powerful statement about the flesh, most particularly about its terrible vulnerability. His passion reminds us of our almost infinite capacity to inflict and suffer hurt. Easter comes as a real relief, as we move away from the uncomfortable physicality of Good Friday. The resurrection can seem almost a pleasant abstraction: we ring bells and surround ourselves with lilies and joyous music as we distance ourselves from Jesus' broken body.

But the risen Christ did not appear to his followers in dreams or visions: he came among them in the homeliness and everydayness of shared walks and meals.

It overwhelms me when I let myself realize that he comes among us still in everydayness. That he still says: "See my hands and my feet, see that it is I myself. Don't avert your eyes from my wounds, either from politeness or disgust. Look at them." He still says: "Put your finger here and see my hands. Reach out your hand and put it in my side. Don't be afraid to touch me. Remember the Incarnation. Remember that I came among you first in human flesh—flesh that can be hungry and be fed, flesh that can be hurt, even be killed. Flesh that can embody God's love."

So he comes among us still, mediated through human flesh. See his hands and his wounded side. Touch him, and see.

Good Friday

Last Good Friday I was invited to preach at a down-town church. Washington was at its most beautiful: the sky was deep blue, puffy white clouds were scud-ding about, and there were blossoms everywhere. The tourist season was just beginning, so the sidewalks were crowded with government employees on their lunch break and camera-laden folk from Joplin, Japan, and all points in between.

I preached in a magnificent old church surrounded by glass-and-steel buildings, then joined the rector and the congregation to walk to the White House and the Mall for the Stations of the Cross. Almost no one noticed us, except for a busload of Japanese tourists, who took our pictures, and a few ordinary Americans who looked a little anxious. I suspect that they feared we would do something loud and tasteless. I wanted to reassure them—"We're Episcopalians!"—but decided that their uncertainty would be good for them.

We ended up back at the church for a prayer. Then the congregation dispersed, and I headed for the sub-way. In the short distance between the church and the Metro station I traveled another Way of the Cross where I encountered three beggars, all women.

A white woman was sitting on a bench directly in front of the church. It was hard to guess her age—she could have been anywhere from thirty to fifty, but she was probably much younger than she looked. Her clothes were shabby, but not ragged, and there was an infinite sadness in her slumped body. For me, she was a visual reproach: I had just come from a carefully executed liturgy with splendid music in a beautiful building, followed by a quite painless, somewhat romanticized act of public witness. Even though it was now three o'clock and I had missed lunch, I was more than well fed. I was dressed in clean if not elegant clothes, and I was on my way to my spacious and pleasant home. Our eyes met, we said hello, and I gave her a dollar. Her look of startled gratitude shamed me even more.

I hadn't gone far before I met an older black woman pushing a shopping cart filled with the detritus of street living. She was heavily dressed, quite possibly wearing her entire wardrobe. She had a scarf pulled over her head, so that her face was barely visible. There was something timeless about her, and a little bit majestic. I pulled out another dollar. She gave me a surprisingly radiant smile and said, "Have a happy Easter, Sweetheart!" Maybe she called everyone Sweetheart, but I'd like to think she meant it.

Then at the street corner just before the subway station, someone called, "Hey, Sister!" By then I had decided that this was my day for encounters with God's poor, and moreover I was in uniform. (In my black suit with a clerical collar and no makeup I looked more like a sister than any of my radical sister-friends.) So I walked over to a middle-aged black woman sitting on a bench. She told me a disjointed story of how her house had burned down in Virginia (just across the river) and how helpful police had advised her that her best course was to leave the neighborhood. So now she and her brother were living in their car in the heart of Washington. Who knows? Maybe she was. Two dollars this time, one for her and—she reminded me—one for her brother. She dismissed me with a cheerful goodbye: "Have a nice day, Sister!"

The gossipy section of the *Washington Post* has a new interest in reporting on celebrity diners out on the town: where they were spotted dining, what they ate, and—most important—how much they tipped. It's clear that fifteen percent is now regarded as stingy and twenty percent will barely do. The big-time spenders who want to look good in tomorrow's paper leave a tip equal to the bill. Is this a form of blackmail? Probably.

I feel blackmailed by the beggars on our street corners. Some of them are con artists and know that they are blackmailing me. I simply assume that I will be duped ten, fifteen, even twenty percent of the time. That doesn't bother me. It's an inevitable part of urban living; I chalk it up to experience.

My real discomfort has deeper roots. It feels like spiritual blackmail. On that Good Friday, I had preached—with some eloquence and real feeling—on how we see the face of the crucified Christ in the world around us, how he intrudes upon our comfort and complacency in all the sick, the needy, the broken and hurting. Despite my carefully crafted sermon, I hadn't planned to meet him in a five-minute walk to the subway.

Not too long ago I felt that I could buy my peace of mind with a quarter. Now a dollar is hardly enough, but it's better than walking away and wondering: was that a con artist who called "Hey, Sister?" or had I turned my back on him?

Life Goes On

He is the Way.
Follow Him through the Land of
    Unlikeness;
You will see rare beasts,
and have unique adventures.*

—*W. H. Auden*

* From "For the Time Being," *Collected Longer Poems* (New York: Random House, 1965), 196–197.

I'm Proud To Be an Eagle

I've never been a refugee, but I love the songs of comfort and homecoming sung to the exiled children of Israel by the Second Isaiah. Maybe something in me is yearning for home when I whisper "yes!" to the promise that "those who wait for the LORD shall renew their strength, they shall mount up with wings like eagles, they shall run and not be weary, they shall walk and not faint" (Isaiah 40:31).

I'm not sure that I have ever seen an eagle. But I have watched hawks. They too are raptors, graceful and powerful, with their own mystery. And I've read up on eagles in my Petersen's guide. And goodness knows, I've studied the eagles on our twenty-five-cent piece.

We are told that we will mount up with wings like eagles. What a picture! Although half of them must be female, I think of eagles as rather masculine birds. It's easier for me to think of myself as a dove, at least in my gentler moments. Or a motherly hen, perhaps. Occasionally, in full academic or ecclesiastical regalia, I might suggest a bird of paradise. But it's difficult to identify with eagles.

Yet we are promised that—if we wait upon the LORD—we shall renew our strength and mount up with wings like eagles. Not earthbound chickens, or even graceful swans. But like eagles! Powerful, majestic, mysterious birds.

Eagles are fierce. Just look at their talons! I wonder:
is it time for me to cultivate fierceness? Not destructive
fierceness, but the single-minded fierceness that can
reflect the love of God. Fierceness in my response to
injustice and cruelty, fierceness in my response to all
that turns me away from love and generosity.

Eagles are steadfast, known for their almost
Benedictine stability. They mate for life and return
again and again to the same nest site. Most of us do not
nest on the side of a cliff; indeed most of us have moved
many times from the house where we were born and
grew up. Our human relationships are not immutable,
and much as the Religious Right might mourn the
passing of the traditional family of mother, father, and
two-point-five children, we know that sometimes
there is health and wholeness in letting go of relationships.

Nevertheless, we can emulate the eagle's steadfast-
ness, resisting change simply for the sake of change,
remaining in our simultaneously precarious and stable
nest. Somewhere St. Clare said, "I have fixed the anchor
of my soul." Our anchors can be fixed and our spiritual
nest on the side of the cliff secure, no matter how grand
or humble our dwelling.

Most importantly, though, eagles have perspective:
with their eagle eyes, they see the big picture. At the
same time, the eagle's vision is keen. She can see and
distinguish tiny things from a great distance. Medieval
bestiaries ascribe almost magical powers to this ability
to discern and distinguish the tiniest significant detail
from a sea of details. My human vision needs the help
of spectacles these days, but eagle vision can be culti-
vated at any age and without the assistance of the ophthalmologist. With eagle eyes, I can appreciate the

sweeping immensity of God's creation and at the same time the wonder of the minuscule, Julian's vision of all creation in "something like a hazel nut" and William Blake's similar vision of the world in a grain of sand:

> To see a World in a Grain of Sand
> And a Heaven in a Wild Flower,
> Hold Infinity in the palm of your hand
> And Eternity in an hour. *

Finally, eagles are an endangered species. I hope that Christians are not in similar peril of extinction, but we need to keep the possibility in our consciousness. If not endangered, we are assuredly less secure in our numbers and indestructibility than pigeons or sparrows! Like the eagle, though, we are strong enough to survive—not with the help and protection of the Sierra Club, but by the grace and with the love of God.

But what really impresses me about eagles is their manner of flight: they let themselves be carried by currents of air. They know when to rest, when to let themselves be lifted up, and when to glide downward. At the same time, they know when to use their powerful wings. They know when to let themselves be carried, and when to achieve by their own efforts. You might say that they know the difference, the balance between action and contemplation. They know how to care and not to care.

We need to know when to work hard, when to use all the force of our powerful wings, when to know that we must work with all our might in the service of others and even—seemingly—just to survive. In eagle parlance, we need to know how to keep ourselves aloft, to keep from plummeting to the ground. We must care about cruelty, ugliness, and death. We must care about

* William Blake, *Selected Poems*, ed. P. H. Butter (London: J. M. Dent & Sons, 1982), 132.

healing, and beauty, and justice. And we must care about the kingdom of God among us. We must care, must be attentive, must be passionate. We must use our keen eyes and strong wings, indeed our fierceness.

And, at the same time, we need to know when to let go and let ourselves be carried. We must be able to let ourselves be carried by the downdrafts and updrafts of the breath of God.

A Golden September Day

September 11, 2001, was a golden day. The air was fresh, cleared of the humidity of a Washington summer, the last roses were blooming on scraggly, leafless bushes, and the big oak trees in my neighborhood were thick with still-green leaves. I was looking forward to a pleasant day in the parish, meeting with people who had come to talk and enjoying the company of my colleagues. Just before I went to the reception area to meet my first appointment, Pattie—who has a small television set in her office—called to me, quietly but urgently, "Come look at this."

A plane had hit just above the middle of one of the towers of the World Trade Center. As I watched in disbelief, I couldn't tell whether it was a large or small plane. This just couldn't be happening. How many times had I traveled between Washington and New York on the shuttle, quick no-frills trips that always reminded me of a bus ride? How many times had I rejoiced at sitting on the left side of the plane so that I could watch the long, skinny Island of Manhattan unfold below me and try to find familiar buildings— the tower of the chapel of the seminary where I had spent so many years, the Empire State Building, the Chrysler Building (which always seemed like a gussied-up smaller version of the Empire State Building), the distinctive slanted roof on the Citicorp Center? And of course the twin towers of the World Trade Center.

"This doesn't makes sense," I said to Pattie. "I've flown that route a million times. There's no way anyone could make a mistake like that." Then, as we watched, the second tower was hit. It was no mistake.

The world changed for me in that few minutes. Or perhaps more accurately, my perception of the world underwent a drastic change, rather like the shifting of the tectonic plates beneath its surface.

I knew, in theory, about the fragility of the fabric of our little lives. I had preached about it, built retreats around the theme of our human transience, and tucked a reminder of our frailty and impermanence wherever appropriate into my writings. I knew, in theory, that I was living in a cocoon of comfort and privilege. I tried, in theory, to remember to give thanks every morning for the reassuring predictability of my days. Even though I never articulated it, I now knew I was living in the self-centered illusion that—whatever might be happening elsewhere in the world or even in the troubled corners of my own city—destruction could never come near me.

I had been missing the point.

There is *nothing* in the Good News of the gospel to assure me of any such thing. There is *nothing* in Jesus' teachings that guarantees my comfortable middle-class life of abundance, where the ongoing problem is not finding enough to eat, but rather holding down the caloric intake. Where I am surrounded by books and beauty. Where my bedroom is cool in the summer and warm in the winter. Where I plan on dying—in the fullness of time, of course—without pain and with sweet dignity. Rather like Melanie of *Gone with the*

Wind, if she had managed to live to a ripe old age. Maybe I will. And, of course, maybe I won't.

In those few moments, everything had changed, and nothing had changed.

As I stood mesmerized by the images on that small television screen, I found myself remembering another September day fifty-one years ago, when—as a wide-eyed twenty-one-year-old fresh out of Kansas and poised to explore the world—I attended Morning Prayer in the tourist-class library of the *Queen Elizabeth I.* The captain led services for first-class passengers, the second mate for those in cabin class. We students and other poor folk had to make do with the purser, impressive enough with his British accent and his impeccable Cunard uniform.

As we knelt—you knelt a lot in those days!—on a floor that tilted beneath us with the movement of the ship, I was acutely conscious of being almost in the middle of a great, gray, cold ocean. I was far from home for the first time in my life. Child of Midwestern farmers and accustomed to having my feet firmly planted on God's stable earth, I had entrusted myself to a ship that had looked mammoth in the New York harbor and now seemed pitifully small. I wasn't frightened, but I was awed as I reflected on my own smallness and powerlessness.

The purser read prayers in the comfortingly archaic language of the *old* Church of England prayer book, and then—still swaying back and forth on our now-aching knees—we sang "Eternal Father, strong to save." It was my first encounter with *Hymns Ancient and Modern.* We sang from tiny, worn little books that had probably worked their way down from first class to us humble folk. I had never heard the hymn before. Even the American version was not relevant to Midwesterners.

Since that first hearing and singing, this old hymn always moves me almost to tears. It is a childlike prayer, reminding me of my ultimate helplessness, reminding me that I am adrift and that my boat is very small.

My life these days is rather like life on the *Queen Elizabeth I*. The pattern of each day is predictable, the company is pleasant, and the food is good. There are no reassuring officers in crisp Cunard uniforms, but there are other signs of benevolent authority. We don't have lifeboat drills, but there are increased security measures at airports.

While I have lost the naive trustfulness of my twenties, it is nevertheless easy to feel safe and even complacent in this abundant corner of God's vineyard. But the events of that golden September day are a reminder of just who I am in God's great scheme of things. I am reminded that I am very small and ultimately powerless. My classy oceanliner is a far cry from the little boat in which Jesus' terrified friends crouched as they were buffeted by wind and waves. My boat is so comfortable and well appointed that sometimes I even manage to persuade myself that it is *terra firma*.

It isn't. It's time to drop to my knees on that shifting deck and whisper or cry out, "O hear us when we cry to Thee for those in peril on the sea." Especially us, right now, whether we find ourselves traveling first class or tourist. Our boat is really very small.

Prayer and Broccoli

I confess great fondness for all vegetables, but especially for broccoli. I love its cool blue-green color, its
crispness, its delicately intricate flowerets, and most
especially its peasant sturdiness. Treated with even
moderate respect it will, unlike some of its more elegant cousins, wait patiently in the refrigerator without
turning brown or going limp. This winter and early
spring, it has been the most abundant and attractive
vegetable at our neighborhood supermarket. So it turns
up in stir fry, in my vegetable-laden pasta sauce, and
quite often all by itself.

A few years ago our forty-first President had the
temerity to malign this worthy member of the crucif-
erous family. He brought down the wrath of us veggie-
crunchy folk upon him: he had denigrated the
nutritional worth of an admirable vegetable. To put it
more bluntly, he had failed to recognize one of God's
gifts.

I try to remember to offer a little prayer of thanksgiving whenever I eat broccoli. At the same time, it is
also an occasion for intercession, as I try to remember
for a moment the people who squat in the fields to
harvest it, the truck driver who hauls it, and the Korean
greengrocer who gets up before dawn to go to the city
market.

This noble-humble vegetable has become for me a symbol, indeed an icon for all the good things I take for granted. It reminds me of all the work of others—tedious, repetitive, sometimes backbreaking work—that keeps me safe, well fed, and comfortable. It reminds me of my dependence on people whom I will never see, many of them very different from me in appearance, education, and lifestyle. It reminds me how much I need those unknown people whom I might—unwittingly—diminish, hurt, or exclude. It reminds me that I am not so self-sufficient as I might like to think.

At the same time, just a look at the crisp vegetable on my plate is a reminder of who I am supposed to be. Jesus said to his friends that "the harvest is plentiful, but the laborers are few" (Matthew 9:37). Hired hands are needed out in the field to reap the harvest. There is a certain romantic charm in this picture, so long as we don't examine it too closely. It recalls Breughel's golden painting of the harvesters stretched out and resting on the stubble amid neat sheaves. And Millet's devout gleaners pausing in their work to pray the *Angelus*. And the old gospel hymn of my younger days, sung lustily by our congregation of city folk who wouldn't know a hoe from a harrow, "We shall come rejoicing, bringing in the sheaves."

But as I meditate on this passage of Matthew's gospel and the broccoli on my plate, I find myself drawn to the harvest laborers of our own time—not the picturesque Flemish peasants in Breughel's painting or Millet's sentimental gleaners, but the real harvest workers of our day.

I shrink from the thought that Jesus is calling me to be a migrant laborer like the itinerant apple pickers who turn up every September in my neighbor's orchard. Can he expect me to stretch and carry until my body cries out for rest, to sweat in the sun and shiver in the rain? To sleep, if I am lucky, in a rundown motel where few travelers would willingly stop? I'm no delicate flower. After all, my forebears were farmers—peasants, to put it bluntly. I know how to work; I've scrubbed my share of floors and toilets. I've fetched and toted along with the best of them. But surely, I'm just a little bit special. Surely I am more than a stoop laborer in a whole field of stoop laborers. There must be plenty of others without my wonderful combination of skills and gifts who can do the hard stuff, who won't mind the long hours and tough conditions, who don't really need a clean mattress and a private bath. Surely, with my impressive résumé, I belong in management.

The Lord of the harvest, however, doesn't seem interested in résumés. We're all invited to sign on at the same payscale. We're invited work long hours, to get tired, to have hurt hands and aching muscles. We're invited to work under pressure of time and the weather. To sign on as a harvest laborer in the fields of the Lord is not to be taken lightly.

Right now my work of writing and teaching absorbs me. I try to remember to give thanks for it each morning and to give it all to God—my thoughts, my words, and my actions. It's easy work because it is the work I love. But my day in the fields isn't over yet. I'm not sure where the Lord of the harvest might send me before the sun goes down. I can only pray for the strength, endurance, and sheer doggedness of a dedicated migrant laborer. It's not my vineyard or field or orchard. I'm just a sojourner in the vineyard, hired on for my little day.

Pruning

Several years ago I was invited to give a retreat based on Jesus' words in John's gospel, "I am the true vine, and my Father is the vinedresser" (John 15:1, RSV; NRSV: "vinegrower"). My heart sank: is there anything new to be said about these words? Almost before I opened my Bible, I dashed off to the local megabookstore to read up on viticulture. I learned a lot!

The growing of grapes is labor intensive, year-round, exacting work, by no means a matter of letting nature take its course. Indeed, the vinegrower seems often to work against nature to create his own order in the vineyard. At every step there is intentionality, decisiveness, and what often looks like ruthlessness to my sentimental eye. Vines may look all alike to the casual observer, but the viticulturist knows each plant, each branch, even each bud on the branch.

One of my authorities startled me in his description of optimum growth conditions: "To produce great wine, the vines must suffer, rather like athletes."[*] In the same vein, another observed: "One viticultural theory is that a struggling vine produces better wine that one that has better growing conditions. If this is true, the reason may be that the struggling vine has smaller berries than the vine growing under more favorable conditions."[†] These small grapes are brighter colored, and their flavor is more intense. Soil that is too rich

---

[*] Jeff Cox, *From Vines to Wines: The Complete Guide to Growing Grapes and Making Your Own Wine* (New York: Harper & Row, 1985).
[†] Robert Weaver, cited by Cox, *From Vines to Wines.*

results in inferior grapes. Hence the plants flourish in the stony soil on steep hillsides where erosion has worn the land down.

The ongoing work of the vinedresser—beyond, of course, great attentiveness to all conditions of growth—is pruning. He knows how many buds are on each vine, which will bear the best fruit, which will bear but not well, and which to pinch away. Like the shepherd who knows each sheep in his flock, for the vinedresser each branch, indeed each bud is an individual. In pruning, a slow start is best—the vinedresser nicks off flower buds for the first two years so that the strength of the vine must go into the root and leaf production.

And he must know what he is doing: "To prune properly—whether to train a young vine or maintain a mature one—it's necessary to understand how a grapevine grows. Otherwise, a vine is an unintelligible jumble of trunks, arms, canes, shoots, leaves, tendrils, and fruit clusters."* There is real intimacy between grower and vine, for each plant is treated as an individual.

Pruning does not kill; rather it promotes good growth and prevents what the experts call "overcropping." An unpruned vine can produce up to one hundred times more buds than are necessary for a good harvest of grapes. The vine's inner urge is toward quantity; the vinegrower seeks quality.

Vineyards are beautiful places. I have walked in many of them—on the steep banks of the Mosel, in the hills around Vienna, and now in the rolling hills of the Blue Ridge. But since that retreat I look at them with new eyes: it's time to stop identifying with the vine grower and see myself as one of the vines. The analogies are clear. When I read how the viticulturist is

---

* Cox, *From Vines to Wines*, 65–66.

called to such intimate awareness of each plant, I thought inevitably of the God for whom the hairs of our head are numbered and to whom we are more precious than sparrows. We are valuable plants, capable of bearing good fruit. But left to our own devices, we aren't worth much. We need the support of a good trellis and the right growing conditions. Most of all, though, we need the attention of the vinedresser. We need careful pruning.

The vineyard in February, leafless and with branches cut back to almost nothing, looks very different from the same vineyard in September, with its generous branches of luxuriant leaves weighted down with ripe fruit. Like the branches on the vine, we need to live through the peaks—the times of obvious growth, flourishing, and fruition—and the valleys—the times of loss and pain, when maybe we feel as if we have been pruned so severely that we are nothing more than a bare, dry stick. We need also to live through the winter times of dormancy, when nothing seems to be happening.

I would rather not be pruned. It looks like much more fun to be one of the wild grapes that I find in the woods, their vines tangled in the host tree and their fruit—what little there is—way up there in the sky somewhere. Nobody tells them what to do. But they aren't worth much, either. If we are to bear good fruit, we must be pruned.

I certainly would not suggest that affliction is divinely ordained and that gratuitous suffering, suffering for its own sake, is good for us. Yet it seems very clear that an untested faith is no faith at all. And that an immature faith may hold much promise, but it is just that—promise. I think getting pruned, getting pinched back is not so much about gratuitous suffering inflicted by a cruel God as about the inevitable losses that accompany faithful living.

We've all been pruned; we've all been pinched back. It's painful. It feels like loss to let go of our tangle of useless branches. Yet such loss—or seeming loss—is an inevitable concomitant of growth, of saying "yes" to God.

Getting pruned and pinched back is about simplicity. The vine left to itself grows lavishly, wildly, and produces a poor crop. We North Americans live in such abundance! Maybe most of us are living in that place where the soil is too rich—certainly, our society encourages us toward wild, lush growth.

There is a certain austerity of a well-tended vineyard. There is also stability, order, and care. We are invited to trust, not to fear the pruning necessary for growth. We can trust because we know our value: the branches are there, held up by their trellis and pruned by the gardener, to bear fruit. And they will, in God's good time.

Sheep

Sheep are the most prominent animals in Scripture. Donkeys do pretty well, dogs get bad press; lions prowl through the Old Testament, majestic and menacing, while cats—their reputation tarnished by their affinity for Egyptians—are nowhere to be found. But sheep seem to meet with divine approval. Sheep turn up in the lectionary, and winsome sheep grace our stained glass windows. Jesus reminds us that he is the Good Shepherd: we know him and he knows us (John 10:14). In other words, sheep are us. This has to be one of the ironies of urban and suburban North American Christianity. There are no sheep grazing in my corner of Northwest Washington, D. C., although for years I worshiped in the Victorian Gothic Chapel of the Good Shepherd and as a child I lustily sang "Savior, like a shepherd lead us."

Yet my own firsthand experience with sheep is limited. From a distance, I have looked at them grazing. For a few days I walked among them on the Isle of Iona and found them skittish and aloof. I have eaten the occasional lamb chop and have a slight allergy to wool.

Most of what I know about sheep is hearsay, undocumented, and not flattering. They are reputed to be stupid, lacking in initiative, and likely to fall over cliffs or entangle themselves in brush. They are not playful.

Lambs have an innocent charm, but the adult animal is stolid and a little boring. Rams are distinguished by their horns, and there may be some variation in color; but the average sheep looks just like the rest of the flock. To look into the face of one sheep is to have seen them all.

I am not really pleased to be grouped with the sheep. In this I suspect that I am not alone. We live in a society that places high value on ingenuity, creativity, and individuality. It is better to be a leader than a follower—can you imagine parents urging their children to be good sheep, to aim for mediocrity in things academic and athletic? We admire people with high levels of energy and a zest for exploration. No, to be a good sheep is not part of the American Dream.

Most significantly, sheep need a shepherd. There is no such thing as an independent or self-made sheep. They need the shepherd if they are to be guided and cared for, and—in dire straits—to be rescued. There is nothing sentimental about this relationship: for the sheep it is a matter of survival, and for the shepherd it is a matter of economy. The sheep are not pets, to be cuddled and cosseted; rather, they are valuable property. The shepherd's treasure, if you will.

Perhaps all sheep look alike to my city-bred eye, but the good shepherd knows his sheep: to him they are individuals. Each one is worthy of his care and attention. Each one is valuable. So in Luke's gospel, when Jesus is trying to give his hearers some idea of God's love for the seemingly insignificant individual, he tells the story of the shepherd who leaves the flock to search for the troublesome stray who has got lost in the wilderness. For all we know, it was a scruffy sheep, the runt of the flock. But the shepherd carries it home, rejoicing.

There are no sheep on the streets of my neighborhood, but I am increasingly and keenly aware of those people whom we so easily turn into sheep, those people who "all look alike," who are indistinguishable to the unloving eye. The boisterous, slightly threatening teenagers who rush onto the subway when school is out at three o'clock, the homeless who warm themselves on sidewalk grates and huddle in doorways, the frail aged lined up in their wheelchairs in nursing home corridors, the caged young men in our jails and prisons—they can become sheep, one like another, and easily replaceable. Or not missed, if one disappears. When I see pictures of refugees, those victims of indescribable suffering, they blur and begin to look alike. Even the individual child, with great pleading eyes and the bloated belly of starvation, begins to look like every other starving child, while the mother holding the body of her dead infant looks like all the other mothers.

I want to turn people into sheep because it is easier that way. It shields me from being touched by the depths of their pain and need, and it helps me deny my kinship with them. It lets me forget that I am a sheep too.

It's quite all right to be a sheep, so long as we pay attention and hear the shepherd's voice. The essential, crucial point is this: the good shepherd knows the sheep. This is not just a matter of a head count; each is of distinct value.

I yearn to be known, and at the same time I fear it. Most of the time, we let ourselves be known by bits and pieces, and we know others in the same way. My husband of nearly half a century thinks that he knows me, my children are sure they have me figured out, my colleagues and students and friends also would claim that they know me. Foolishly, I think I know myself. Even as I want to be known, I want to be known on my own terms—a carefully constructed and edited version, not as a sheep who gets lost, falls off cliffs, and gets hung up in the brambles. Certainly not as a sheep who can't find her own way.

To be known, fully known, is not possible in our human relationships, but it is the foundation of our relationship with Christ. To be known, fully known, is both painful and profoundly comforting. It is to accept the humble status of sheep, to let the masks and defenses drop away, and to let ourselves be carried on the shepherd's shoulders and occasionally poked by his staff. It means sometimes to be thwarted—the edge of that cliff doesn't look too dangerous, and I wasn't going to wander very far, honest!— and sometimes to be shut in a pen. It means to listen for the shepherd's voice and to rejoice that he knows which one I am, in this great, blundering, well-intentioned, sheepish flock.

The Collect for Purity, the prayer of preparation before the Eucharist, is the prayer of the grateful sheep:

> Almighty God, to you all hearts are open, all desires known, and from you no secrets are hid: Cleanse the thoughts of our hearts by the inspiration of your Holy Spirit, that we may perfectly love you, and worthily magnify your holy Name; through Christ our Lord. (*Book of Common Prayer,* 355)

Amen!

Is That Bush on Fire?

It must have begun as an ordinary day. Moses, whose life up to now has surely known its ups and downs, has to be grateful for its blessed ordinariness. The rescued offspring of an enslaved Israelite, reared in the royal household, he is now a fugitive, dependent on his father-in-law and tending his flock. At this point, he does not seem a likely candidate to do God's work in a big way.

So there he is, in the middle of nowhere, surrounded by somebody else's goats or sheep. I have never tended a flock—although I have looked after chickens—but I imagine that it would be tedious work, with long stretches of time when nothing happens and there is nothing very interesting to look at, at least until night when the stars come out.

Then "the angel of the LORD appeared to him in a flame of fire out of a bush; he looked, and the bush was blazing, yet it was not consumed" (Exodus 3:2). Was it a big bush? A little bush? It might have been just a tiny patch of dry, scruffy vegetation that *could* have ignited spontaneously in the midday sun. Or it might have been a breathtaking, terrifying conflagration with flames and smoke reaching to the sky. Whatever it was, it got Moses' attention: "I must turn aside," he tells himself, "and look at this great sight, and see why the bush is not burned up" (3:3).

Moses has seen something that he doesn't understand. Something completely out of the ordinary. This can happen, even to ordinary folk—perhaps overwhelmingly or perhaps just at the edge of our peripheral vision, when we glimpse something that astounds us, draws us closer, and compels us to leave off what we are doing and turn aside. I recall the summer afternoon in the Blue Ridge when I moseyed into the kitchen to put my coffee cup in the sink and there, just at the edge of my vision, barely perceptible but nonetheless arresting, I glimpsed a sinuous black something under the kitchen table. It wasn't God (at least so far as I know) but a six-foot-long black snake that had slipped into the house. It got my attention!

My black snake—physical, literal, and quite embodied—was hard to miss, but I have to ask myself: How many burning bushes have I missed? How many times have I kept my eyes resolutely on the sheep and goats, persuading myself that the wisps of smoke and darts of flame were mere illusions or distractions? How many people—good, well-intentioned people like me—spend their whole lives as conscientious herdsmen and never notice a bush that is flaming away right under their noses?

When I read this story last week—a story I have known or thought I knew since childhood—I noticed a sentence that I had not seen before: "When the LORD saw that he had turned aside to see, God called to him out of the bush: 'Moses, Moses!'" (3:4).

It sounds as if God is as surprised as Moses. And this makes me wonder: how long had that bush been burning in the arid solitude of the desert before anyone noticed it? How many herdsmen and travelers had passed by without a second glance? It's as if God is there, accessible, almost lying in wait, hoping to be noticed.

So God calls Moses by name, and Moses gives the right answer, the only answer we can give when we hear God call our names: "Here I am."

This is one of the great stories of vocation, of call—when God invades our consciousness and calls us by name. To be called by name can be flattering—ah, I am special! I have been singled out for attention! Or it can be alarming—why am I being paged, of all the hundreds or maybe thousands of people in this busy airport? Perhaps I am being upgraded, or maybe the airport police have singled me out as the dangerous person I really am.

Regardless of the circumstances, to hear our name called gets our attention.

At least according to this story, maybe we have to stop, move a little closer, let go of our distractions—all those wayward sheep and goats—before we hear our name called clearly. Even if we are ready to dismiss the burning bush as a curiosity, something one might find on the Discovery Channel, to hear our name called unexpectedly stops us in our tracks. It gets our attention. Even when the caller is a mere human—one of the distorted voices over an airport PA system or the counter person at Blimpie's telling us that we can pick up our sandwich—our existence has been validated. We are. We are known.

But here Moses hears the voice of God. This would be a good place for the story to end: God and Moses have found each other, and that should be enough, but as they say in those late-night television pitches for omni-purpose kitchen gadgets—wait! There's more!

There comes a warning: Come no closer! Take off your shoes. This is holy ground. That's a good reminder of the power and ultimate unknowability of the God who nevertheless knows us and loves us in spite of ourselves. We can grow almost too comfortable and easy, almost casual in our relationship with the high voltage God whom the twentieth-century theologian Rudolf Otto termed "a tremendous and fascinating mystery."

So we must take off our shoes, remembering that we are of the earth, *humus,* before we come closer. Moses hears the voice of God from his own place of smallness and imperfection, deeply aware that God is God and that he is not God. And God's message then (and maybe now) was one of compassion, challenge, and promise, all enmeshed and tangled together. Yes, Moses' people are promised deliverance, abundance, and safety—but Moses has to do the work. He must accept the terrible burden of partnership with the God who speaks from the bush.

And quite naturally, Moses feels inadequate: "Who am I that I should go to Pharaoh and bring the Israelites out of Egypt?" (3:11). We know how the story ends—we have read the book and seen the movie. (Though I don't imagine Moses bore the slightest resemblance to Charlton Heston.) What is being asked of him: the impossible. Or the absurd.

Even though God promises to be with him, Moses needs more assurance. So he asks, as I most certainly would be tempted to ask: Who should I say is calling? I AM WHO I AM is not really a satisfactory answer, but it is all that Moses gets. God remains a mystery, to be approached with awe. Jesus, though, gives us another name—Abba—and invites us to come closer. Both names are the right ones.

I'm trying to keep an eye out for burning bushes—maybe at the neighborhood playground just down the street, maybe at Wal-Mart, maybe in my own backyard. I'm trying to listen, just in case my name is called. And I hope to be ready to slip off my sturdy sandals or my sensible grandmotherly shoes—depending on the weather—as I draw closer to the mystery.

It's Time for an Onion Sandwich

My maternal grandmother—the other Margaret Adah—was a storyteller. Long before there were storytelling workshops and conferences, long before people had brochures and business cards printed extolling their narrative skills, she told stories. Because the adults in the household had heard all the stories too many times, I fear that I was her only audience. I could listen endlessly and knew instinctively that much of the richness of oral narration lies in repetition. So I would hear the same story over and over again, with not a word altered, in much the same way that I now listen to the same CD of a Beethoven piano concerto over and over again. Even if not a word or a note changed, there was and is always something new to hear.

My grandmother was born on a farm in Illinois, right at the end of the Civil War. Her forebears were New Englanders, lured west by the railroad and the promise of good land. She was educated in a one-room country school, maybe for six years, maybe for a few more. I think she must have loved words the way I do. All her life she was hungry for them and hungry for stories. She owned only a few books, which she read over and over. Otherwise she depended on her own memories for her stories.

In many ways, she was a difficult woman, impatient and—I suspect—angry at the smallness of her world.

But I as her namesake and the small one in the family knew her generous and gentle side. It was always a treat to sit with her while she sewed and listen to her stories. My favorite was "The Little Girl and the Onion Sandwich."

My grandmother told the story slowly and sparely, and my imagination filled in the details. The child was at the point of death. Her loved ones had gathered around her bedside. I could see the farmhouse sickroom, the distraught parents, and the poor little girl—who was no doubt beautiful and good—slipping away. There was no hope. So the grief-stricken parents decided to give her anything she wanted since she would surely be dead by the next day.

When they asked her what she wanted, she rallied a bit and said, "An onion sandwich." The request took the parents by surprise, but since there was nothing to lose, her mother fixed the sandwich. Here my grandmother's style grew expansive as she described ingredients and preparation with a skill and subtlety that a *New York Times* food critic would envy. It was clear that the onion sandwich was delectable!

For a moment, the dramatic tension of the story was forgotten as she lapsed into her pedagogic mode. She was, after all, my exacting instructor in cross-stitch and crochet, pastry-making and chicken-plucking. A good teaching moment was not to be ignored.

First, a thin slice of day-old homemade bread. Of course, only homemade bread was available on a nineteenth-century Illinois farm, and day-old was somehow considered more wholesome. The bread was spread with butter, not too much and not too little. Then a perfect onion, sliced very thin. I could almost see the pale translucent slices. Finally, just a dash of salt and pepper.

The parents offered the sandwich to the sick child, sure that she would reject it. Instead, she ate every bite and recovered at once!

I confess that since childhood this story has always been entangled in my mind with Luke's account of the healing of Jairus's daughter (Luke 8:41–42, 49–56). As a child, I could watch the story unfold in my imagination. I could picture Jesus arriving with his friends at a frame house on a Midwestern farm and reassuring the distraught parents: "She is not dead, but sleeping." And when he commanded that she be given "something to eat," I was sure that her mother produced an onion sandwich, just as delicious and restorative as the one in my grandmother's story.

Both stories are about hope when there is no hope. In my grandmother's version, the humble onion sandwich is a remedy for the irremediable. It lives in my memory as a symbol of unexpected restoration at that darkest moment when everything feels lost. Now and then I mutter to myself, when I feel hard-pressed, "It's almost time for an onion sandwich." But these are words to be uttered with caution and only *in extremis*. They are too powerful to waste on a minor illness or a canceled flight or an overcrowded schedule.

I'm saving them for when I really need them.

Moving Through the Wilderness

Several years ago, a parish asked me to lead off its Lenten study series by ruminating on "wilderness" during the Sunday morning adult education forum. This was an urban and urbane group of people, well groomed and prosperous. Almost all of them enjoyed spacious houses, handsome cars, and equally handsome children. They led quite orderly if busy lives. So it was hard for me to think of them and wilderness in the same sentence—unless, of course, some of the more venturesome signed on for a pricey Outward Bound program. For these folk, any encounter with the wilderness would be a kind of tourist experience, after San Francisco, Cancun, and Prague had lost their luster.

By graced coincidence, while I was pondering my assignment, I spent a few days of retreat in a Benedictine monastery. Most meals were silent, but one of the brothers read aloud while everyone else ate and studiously avoided eye contact with their neighbors. When I first began retreating to monasteries for rest and recreation, I had expected a heavy dose of pious verbiage along with my soup so it was quite a surprise to learn that the brothers listen to all sorts of books at meal-time—history, biography, memoirs, and travel. At the same time, I learned not to become heavily invested in the outcome of the story. The reader stops abruptly when the prior rings a little bell; and if you are staying for only a day or so, you depart with a fascinating fragment or two of a substantial work.

On this particular visit, the dinner reading was from *Undaunted Courage,*★ the detailed and vivid account of the Lewis and Clark expedition. I found myself listening to the story of their trek through the unknown as a metaphor for the spiritual journey. So I spent the remainder of the retreat thinking about the wilderness, literal and spiritual, simultaneously forbidding and beguiling. In that warm, safe place high above the Hudson River I gave myself over to imaginings of traversing desert places, fording wild rivers, searching for hidden mountain passes, and always wondering what lay ahead. I wondered whether the travelers on the expedition were frightened or exhilarated, or maybe both at the same time. Whether they let themselves remember that they would have to retrace their steps once they had achieved their goal. Whether they felt free or coerced, bored, fatigued, or angry. Whether some days they wished that they had never set out.

Since old teachers never die, I checked out "wilderness" in the concordance in the monastery library, where I found literally hundreds of scriptural references to wilderness or desert. I remembered movies and pictures and bad novels. I remembered my grandmother's stories of her Uncle Sam, nearly perishing in the California desert in the quest for gold. I recalled Abram's setting forth from Haran and relived Hagar's banishment to the wilderness of Beer-Sheba. I could see in memory a map from my Old Testament class at seminary, showing the absurdly convoluted wanderings of the Exodus. I pictured John the Baptist, emerging disheveled and cantankerous from the wilderness of Judea, and I remembered Jesus' forty days of fasting and

---

★ Stephen E. Ambrose, *Undaunted Courage: Meriwether Lewis, Thomas Jefferson, and the Opening of the American West* (New York: Simon & Schuster, 1996).

temptation in the desert. Visions of wilderness danced in my head!

What makes a wilderness? It is, first of all, trackless; there are no highways, and even reliable footpaths are hard to find. The landscape is challenging: distances are great, seemingly infinite; mountains are forbidding; and streams are turbulent. The traveler is exposed to extremes of heat and cold and may well be hungry or thirsty. The wilderness is uninhabited, or at least it looks that way. There are often people and certainly animals who are at home in the wasteland, but they reveal themselves reluctantly if at all. Are they friends or foes, welcoming or threatening? Each encounter is an adventure, possibly dangerous, but possibly an occasion of celebration and generosity. But along with the adventure, there is tedium and plain hard work, to move ahead and sometimes just to survive.

What impels us to enter the wilderness? Lewis and Clark were explorers, motivated by intellectual curiosity and a commission from the government. My great-great Uncle Sam was sure that he would find a fortune and never have to work again. The Israelites were fleeing from slavery; when they reached the inevitable point of no return on their journey, they looked back longingly on the security and relative comfort of bondage. Jesus was driven by the Spirit to encounter his deepest self.

So the journey through the wilderness can be a pioneering expedition or an escape. It can also be an occasion to encounter God or God's messengers. Certainly, it contains the promise of a meeting with the unexpected, perhaps a brush with the Holy Spirit. We need undaunted courage as we trek through life, seeking to know the will of God for us, even though we will not plod across the Great Plains or scale the Rockies. We need our courage to be open to the Holy Spirit who drives us into the wilderness and at the same time leads us out of it. We need our courage to look deeply into ourselves, to engage our minds and hearts in study, and to pray boldly.

I said something like this to my friends in the parish hall. There was no time for conversation—the bell was already ringing for the eleven o'clock service. I found myself wondering what all the big and little wildernesses represented in that room might have looked like—beautiful, challenging, hostile, menacing, inviting, irresistible, or commanding. I wondered what they experienced as they traversed them, whether they were able to name and recognize them as holy places.

If Only You Would. . . . Yes, But. . . .

> When Jesus saw him lying there and knew
> that he had been there for a long time, he said
> to him, "Do you want to be made well?"
> The sick man answered him, "Sir, I have no
> one to put me into the pool when the water
> is stirred up; and while I am making my way,
> someone else steps down ahead of me."
>
> *(John 5:6–7)*

I misspent my youth in the movies, absorbing among other things the biblical extravaganzas of Cecil B. DeMille. I'm not sure whether that's a help or hindrance in reading Scripture, but the unbidden pictures are always vivid. So whenever I read the story of the healing by the Sheep Gate, the scene comes alive on the inner screen of my imagination. It's a crowded scene—all kinds of people and domestic animals and, of course, "many invalids—blind, lame, and paralyzed"—gathered around the pool. I'd like to think the pool was crystal clear, cool and inviting; but then I remember all the sick bodies that have been immersed in it, and I suspect it looks a little more like a stagnant pond in a neglected city park. It is reputed to have mysterious curative properties, although I notice that the bit about the periodic appearance of an angel of the Lord has been relegated to a footnote in the New Revised

Standard Version of the Bible. So maybe it's a miraculous pool, and maybe it's just a pool.

The sick and the impaired have gathered for a kind of race or lottery: whoever gets into the water first will be healed of whatever disease he had. This is not a pleasant picture; instead, it suggests a rough and degrading scramble, rather like the cruel game of tossing a handful of coins into a crowd of desperate beggars for the pleasure of seeing them tussle.

We don't know what was wrong with the nameless man singled out by Jesus; but it is clear that his mobility is impaired, since he can't move fast enough to compete. And he is without friends or family, for he complains that there is no one to help him at the magic moment. He has been ill for thirty-eight years, probably for most of his life. Has he ever been well? Does he know what it is to be well?

Jesus asks, "Do you want to be made well?" This seems an absurd question: the man has somehow dragged himself to a place known for its curative powers and has been lying beside the healing waters for "a long time." He must want to be healed. But his response reflects the ambivalence many of us feel about accepting wholeness: without answering directly, the sick man explains how he has been impeded—he has no one to help him, and other people always push ahead of him to get to the water.

We have to *want* wholeness, even when it brings difficulty, pain of a different kind, and new burdens. It must have been miserable lying beside the pool. (My imagination always adds swarms of flies to the scene.) At the very least, the sick man must have endured tedium and isolation in the midst of a crowd. After a few days, weeks, or maybe years of trying to get into the pool first, perhaps he has stopped trying in earnest and accepted his defeat. Perhaps a ritual of just going through the motions has become his daily routine. Then no one can criticize him for want of trying; he is doing all the right things. Surely he wants to be healed, but things just aren't going his way.

But however uncomfortable and bleak as waiting endlessly by the pool might have been, it might well have been safer, more attractive than accepting healing. To accept healing is to accept the reality of radical change, to accept the fullness of our humanity.

It is tempting to read gospel accounts of healing as "happily-ever-after" stories, ending with the restoration of health and wholeness. It is easy to forget that healing can be difficult, frightening, and challenging. When the beggar Bartimaeus asked to receive his sight, did he know how much his blindness had protected him from pain and ugliness, how it had shielded him from really knowing the world around him? Being healed restored him to full participation and accountability in the human family.

Similarly, this nameless man is both shielded and depleted by his illness. No one expects anything of him, and at least he knows where he is. There can be no surprises, lying there waiting for the angel to trouble the waters and knowing that he isn't going to be one of the lucky ones.

I thought of the man lying beside the pool not long ago when I was struck down by one of those twenty-four-hour afflictions, not serious but total while it lasts. What a relief it was to be forced by high temperature and aching bones to take to my bed, without apology for all the things left undone! Even as I protested—to myself as much as to others—my eagerness to be up and doing, a tempting little inner voice whispered seductively about the pleasure of dropping out, the luxury of unaccountability, and the bland safety of my relative helplessness. Lying in bed watching reruns on television is hardly the same as lying beside the pool of Bethzatha, but I had a glimpse of the latter's perils and temptations.

The sick man's ambivalent, self-justifying response reminds me of a popular self-help book of the 1960s, *Games People Play.*★ The author described the phenomenon of "'If only you would. . . .'—'Yes, but. . .'" in which the helping person suggests quite reasonable ways of moving toward wholeness. The troubled or suffering person counters each proposal with a reason why it just won't work. To be human is to be ambivalent: we can want and not want at the same time. We can seek healing and resist it. We can drag ourselves to the poolside and manage to avoid the last crucial steps—because no one will help us or because other people get there first. If only you would. . . . Yes, but. . . .

Fortunately, Jesus does not play games. He is brisk and wastes no words: "Stand up, take your mat, and walk." The man obeys. And he never does step into that pool!

★ Eric Berne, M.D., *The Games People Play* (New York: Ballentine Books, 1996).

Waxed Skis

Jesus wasn't easy on his friends. Just in case they got too comfortable following him, he reminded them of the cost:

> If any want to become my followers, let them deny themselves and take up their cross daily and follow me. For those who want to save their life will lose it, and those who lose their life for my sake will save it. What does it profit them if they gain the whole world, but lose or forfeit themselves? (Luke 9:23–25)

This story appears in the gospels of Matthew, Mark, and Luke. After Jesus' friends have recognized him as the Messiah, he foretells his own suffering, death, and resurrection. And finally he sets forth the terms of the contract—the cost of following him. It's not cheap, and it's not easy. We are told that if we want to follow him, we must deny ourselves and, in the words of the New English Bible, "leave self behind." To our contemporary ears, this sounds like bad advice, dangerous to our mental health. That precious self that we have worked so hard to develop, to bring to some sort of maturity, must be let go. Denied.

We North Americans are an extraordinarily self-absorbed people. Our mega-bookstores are filled with aisles of books on self-improvement, self-discovery, self-defense, and self-awareness. My ancient Webster's dictionary offers four closely written pages of hyphenated words beginning with "self." I'm sure that a newer edition would have even more.

Advertisements for all sorts of products and services exhort us to care for ourselves, indeed to indulge ourselves with everything from expensive hair coloring— *I color my hair with L'Oreal; I'm worth it* (actually, I don't; it's too much trouble)—to luxury ice cream and fast food restaurants—*You deserve a break today,* so go to McDonald's.

For many the concern with our physical self borders on obsession. Not long ago I read an article in one of my beloved supermarket magazines about a woman who held age at bay by working out vigorously for fourteen hours a week. She looked terrific! Then I did my math and realized that she was devoting two full working days a week to maintenance of her body. It was an incredible feat of asceticism, indeed self-denial, in service of self. I'm not sure I know many people (except maybe members of religious orders) who pray that rigorously.

That scale and intensity of our preoccupation with ourselves would baffle our great-grandparents or residents of the so-called Third World. For the first time in history, we pay people to listen while we talk about ourselves, exploring the hidden corners of our psyches and scrutinizing our motives and relationships. The self is nurtured, cosseted—and sometimes loathed. But, encouraged by the demands of a consumer society, we make that self the center of our universe. That's who we are. How we are. Very aware and protective of ourselves.

And here is Jesus, telling us to let that carefully nurtured self go, to abandon ourselves. This requirement for discipleship seems at first glance to fly in the face of other things he has said—his reassurance that we are known and loved by the God who sees each sparrow's fall and that we are infinitely worth more than the flowers of the field and the birds of the air. It seems, too, to contradict the Great Commandments: to love the Lord your God with all your heart, soul, strength, and mind; and to love your neighbor as yourself. Made in God's image, we are expected, indeed commanded to love ourselves.

And then to leave that self behind.

I think that the contradiction is more apparent than real. First of all, of course, we need to know what we are giving up. We need to know who we are. To sort ourselves out, as it were. To know which are the idols that distract and divert us from God and which are the icons, the windows to God. We need to see clearly where our attention and energy are centered.

To embrace our identity in Christ, we need to know and recognize the false, shallow self, the self that lacks generosity and vision, the self that resolutely refuses to move God-ward. We need to see it for what it is and then bit by bit to strip away all those bits that sully and impede us.

But that's not all: we need to recognize as well our true, best, deepest self—to love it, and then to be ready to let even that go. That self is precious. It is the fruit of prayer, joy, sorrow, thought, love, grace, and seeking. Jesus is not saying that we are not valuable. So first we must know, love, and value that self—and then let it go.

That seems like a wildly risky thing to do. It reminds me of my one attempt at skiing, decades ago in the cheapest resort in Austria. It was cheap because there was no lift. I excelled at plodding up the mountainside, but my speedy descent was another matter. I was too conservative, too cautious, indeed too scared to launch myself boldly in flight. People from Kansas just don't hurl themselves off mountaintops. But one night, unbeknownst to me, the instructor waxed my skis. I still remember the exhilaration of hurtling down the mountain, watching the trees fly by and somehow knowing that it was all right, that at the very worst I would find myself inelegantly upended in a snow bank. But instead I sailed along with a certain grace and arrived at the bottom of the slope with both feet on the ground.

Physically, I have never recaptured that experience. Spiritually, I think I glimpse it when I let myself reflect on Jesus' command to let go, to stop holding on, and to abandon ourselves. There can be nothing half-hearted in this relinquishing of self. With unclenched fists and with shoulders back we leap off into the unknown. We let the old self go in the promise that we will receive something better, that even our best, carefully constructed and carefully cosseted self can be an impediment to our radical freedom in Christ. The saints have known this through the centuries. They have been willing to let go, seemingly of everything, and then to emerge more human, more real, more alive than ever as they embrace the freedom of following Christ.

Daily I am sustained by an old prayer that speaks of God as an abyss of love, an image filled with beauty and terror. An abyss, after all, can be a frightening place—it is so deep, its sides are so steep. To plummet into its depths is to lose all control and to risk oblivion.

But the abyss of God's love is different. It promises us safety. Even as we let go and lose ourselves in the plunge, we know that we will not be lost. We will be caught and held, surrounded and embraced by that unfathomable love.

Planting the Apple Tree

And if I knew the world would end tomorrow,
I would nevertheless plant my apple tree.

A long time ago, in what seems like another life, I taught German language to university undergraduates. For most of these young people it was their first encounter with the mysteries and rigor of grammar. They had been speaking their native English with blithe unawareness of the structure underlying it. Our encounter with the subjunctive mood came late in the semester, well after mastery of straightforward statements, questions, and commands. The subjunctive is a mood, not really part of our consciousness as English-speakers, but an enigmatic presence in the language of my paternal forebears. It deals with wishes, conditional utterances of all sorts, and those circumstances where the speaker might wish to distance himself from the content of his utterances.

In the section of our textbook dealing with "subjunctive statements contrary to fact," we read this sentence: *"Und wenn ich wuesste, dass die Welt morgen unterginge, so pflanzte ich doch meinen Apfelbaum."* Grammar books in any language are notoriously dull, rarely a source of literary beauty or spiritual insight. Yet this little sentence, attributed to Martin Luther, has stuck in my mind for decades. I've never encountered it anywhere else and confess that I haven't done the scholarly work of tracking it down through his voluminous writings. Maybe he never even said it. But it told me something I needed to hear, and if I knew that Brother Martin had never said it, I would nevertheless be grateful for this insight.

The sentence is "contrary to fact" because he's reasonably sure that the world won't end tomorrow. There is, of course, always the possibility that it *will* so it's very good to have a contingency plan. Perhaps it is our shared ethnicity that makes me so responsive to this prudent foresight; the mindset of *carpe diem* and "devil take the hindmost" is contrary to our somber Northern nature.

If I knew the world would end tomorrow, I would nevertheless plant my apple tree. Or at least a daffodil. And if I thought there might be just a *little* more time, why not lay the foundation of a cathedral? Or endow a scholarship? Or take a world cruise? Or maybe just do nothing at all and wait for the inevitable to happen?

To plant an apple tree is an act of hope. It is a joyous shout of *l'chaim!* and a quiet reminder that life is to be lived, right down to the last minute. One of the foundational truths of the hospice movement, as articulated by Dame Cecily Saunders, is the fact that the dying are not dead, but living. This is so simple as to seem self-evident, yet it is easy to forget. We are all dying—sooner or later. The world *could* end tomorrow, even though we made it safely past the dramatic moment of midnight 1999/2000. We might blow ourselves up, or that final day—foretold by deranged prophets on street corners and in subway cars—might be upon us. At the very least, our own little world is frail and transient, no matter how vigorous we might be feeling at the moment.

But in the meantime, here we are! Physically, we may be diminished. I'm not sure that I can ride a bicycle anymore, and I'm not about to find out. Professionally, we may have lost interest in fancy titles and having the corner office with the best view. Lately I've been happily ensconced in an eight-by-twelve former storage closet—it's just amazing what a few beloved icons and a couple of lamps can do for the atmosphere! We may have whittled down our list of passionate causes. I have become very selective about which bridge I will die on, not from indifference to injustice but because the preciousness of time has made me a little more discriminating. The world is getting smaller and bigger, simultaneously, but I know very well that I, who was never so big as I thought, am getting smaller.

I see a clear difference between living in foolish and unhealthy denial—in the blatantly false conviction that I am indestructible and impervious to the ravages of age and disease—and the hopeful state that encourages us to plant our apple trees so long as we can totter out to the orchard and dig a modest hole.

But why an apple tree?

Apple trees are sturdy and long-lived, bearing fruit right down to the last. Even moribund, scraggly trees provide a feast for bears, deer, and raccoons. They are at their best when they stay close to the ground. A tall, spindly apple tree isn't much good to anyone; they thrive on drastic pruning that keeps them broad and dense.

And an apple tree bears the most humble of fruits. Lately I've noticed the introduction of new varieties, as if our growers want to compete with the other exotic newcomers that were not around in my childhood—Kiwi fruit and Chilean grapes in mid-winter, lychee nuts and clementines. But there is nothing better than a Virginia Stayman, fresh picked and bought at a roadside stand. Its appearance is unpretentious—not a brilliant glossy red, but rather a little rusty-looking—and its flavor is a foretaste of heaven.

I've been blessed to enjoy the proximity of an apple orchard for a long time. My neighbor, who does the work of planting, pruning, and harvesting, graciously permits me to walk among his trees in all seasons. I had always taken their springtime beauty for granted; a tree in full blossom is enveloped in a fragrant cloud of pale pink. Similarly, a tree at harvest time is a sign of God's abundance, looking almost like a child's drawing in its symmetry and bold color. The surprise, for me, was to realize the beauty of the apple tree in its winter bareness. Maybe Shakespeare had this in mind when he wrote about trees as "bare ruined choirs," for the tracery of the branches is delicate and intricate, not a dull gray but—seen from a distance—tinged with a faint purple.

Finally, when its fruitful days are past, the wood makes hot fires and sweet smoke.

The world probably won't end tomorrow, but I'm thinking about planting an apple tree. Just in case.